SHIVA LINGAM

The 12 Jyotir Lingams of India
The Mt. Kailash - Manasarovar Yatra
The Athi Rudra Maha Yagna

Irene M Watson

SHIVA LINGAM

First Edition 2007

Copyright © Irene M Watson

Irene Margaret Watson
P. O. Box 3329
Nedlands. W.A. 6009
Australia
email: imw@inner-view.com.au
www.globaltransformations.com

ISBN 81-87694-21-1

Printed and bound in India by Vishruti Prints

Books by the same Author:
Who Am I Really? Vols I, II & III

The Shiva Lingam

Rameshwar Lingam

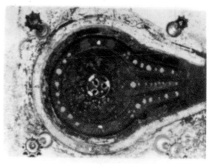

Tryambakeshwar Lingam

Srisailam Lingam

Ghrisheshwar Lingam

Bhimashankar Lingam

Omkareshwar Lingam

Mahakaleshwar Lingam

Somnath Lingam

Nageshwar Lingam

Vishwanath Lingam

Vaidyanath Lingam

Kedarnath Lingam

9-20th August 2006
The Athi Rudra Maha Yagna

Dedicated with love to

Lord Shiva – Sri Sathya Sai Baba

TABLE OF CONTENTS

The 12 Jyothir Lingams

Mt. Kailash & Manasarovar Yatra

The Athi Rudra Maha Yagna

FOREWORD

The worship of Shiva in the Form of the Lingam is an extremely ancient practice, which can be traced back to the times of The Ramayana.

Shiva is the first of the Trinity Gods and represents Creation, Sustenance, and Dissolution – Brahma, Vishnu and Rudra – Shiva.
It is said that Shiva is one in whom The Universe merges after dissolution, before the next cycle of Creation.

Shiva is worshipped in Anthropomorphic Form – Human Body, and in the 'form' of the Lingam.
The Lingam Form of Shiva is commonly found in places of worship and Temples throughout India.
The Human Form of Shiva is more commonly worshipped during celebrations and festivals.

The worship of The Divine Feminine or Shakti is also an ancient Indian and Nepalese custom.

THE 12 JYOTIR LINGAMS are the most *sacred* of all Lingams in India / Bharat, and extend from the extreme north, south, east and west.

They are manifestations of the Lord of Kailasa and the Universe. Shiva and Parvathi are the Universal Father and Mother.

The Lingams were inaugurated by Lord Shiva in sequence 1-12: Somnath, Srisailam, Mahakaleshwar, Omkareshwar, Vaidyanath, Bhimashankar, Rameshwar, Nageshwar, Vishwanath, Tryambakeshwar, Kedarnath and Grishneshwar. All individual Lingams and Temples have their very own *specific* energy, qualities and functions.

A Pilgrimage and Darshan of the 12 Jyotir Lingams will help you to lead a virtuous life, by eliminating the bad qualities of Man, and guide Humanity towards the path of Truth and Righteousness, to reach the goal of Liberation.

The path travelled on *this* particular Pilgrimage was slightly different to the normal route undertaken, and not advisable - due to the extremely high energy, frequency and vibration shifts, resulting in molecular imbalance and changes in consciousness.

The Jyotir Lingams were visited in the sequence:
Rameshwar, Srisailam, Bhimashankar, Tryambakeshwar, Grishneshwar, Omkareshwar, Mahakaleshwar, Nageshwar, Somnath, Vishwanath, Vaidyanath and Kedarnath.

The Energies of the individual 12 Jyotir Lingams were laced together throughout India, and then tied loosely together at Kedarnath, on completion of this part of the journey.

The Energy Cords were then taken to Mt. Kailash in Tibet, where they were looped around the mountain during The Parikrama, or three-day walk around the base of Mt. Kailash, which included the 56 km trek through the Dolma-la Pass.

The Energy Cords were then tightened or loosened, individually or collectively as per Lord Shiva's wishes.

Only after completion of the holy Mt. Kailash and Manasarovar Pilgrimage, did the importance of the Lingam Work begin to manifest, and the realisation that it was *this* work that would perpetuate the 11 Day Athi Rudra Maha Yagna.

This journey will ultimately help in the upliftment of Humanity by facilitating The Divine Feminine – Shakti Energy. Thereby raising Conscious Awareness and evoking great and wondrous Planetary Change, and the long awaited attainment of World Peace.

The book is written in a diarised format, conversational in theme at times, between the author and Sri Sathya Sai Baba or Lord Shiva.
As a silent listener to the 'Voice' of God, the author was *firmly* instructed in regard to all aspects of the entire journey.

Om Sai Ram

Guru Pournima, 2007

Swami read this book during the week 16th July, 2007 and asked that it be published immediately. He said 'the contents of this book are *more* important than anything else.'
However still confronted by my ego, I thought His signature on the book was *more* important.

Days later He then said 'the contents of this book are *more* important than MY SIGNATURE!'
He blessed the book again and said 'Very Happy, Very Happy'

It was only then I released more remnants of 'My Ego'.

INTRODUCTION TO
SHIVA-SHAKTI

This book describes a spiritual journey to the twelve major lingams in India, as well as to Mount Kailash. Unlike the many forms ascribed to God by humans, Sathya Sai Baba tells us that the lingam is a form assumed by the divine. In particular, it is a form assumed by the Masculine Divine, or Shiva.

Shiva does not exist alone, however: Shiva and Shakti, the Masculine and Feminine Divine, are fully intertwined. Although theoretically separable, they are in fact never separated as long as Creation endures. Together they form the Basis of Creation, provide the Energy that runs Creation, and direct and manage Creation. In order to do all this and much more, each is empowered with several interdependent functions. They carry out these functions in seamless harmony.

Among the functions of the Feminine, or Mother, is the cleansing of darkness. Such 'darkness' includes sadness, doubt, mistakes, the down-dragging tendencies such as anger, greed and envy; and all the countless traits, states and actions that beings ask God to remove or forgive. Cleansing occurs when an arc of such darkness connects with an arc of crackling white Light, to form a full circle. The darkness is thereby pulled out and replaced with Light, or other Divine Energies such as love, peace or bliss. Sai Baba describes this as negative and positive poles meeting; the negative from created beings, the positive, from the divine.

This meeting of the positive and negative poles is accomplished through faith. Faith in the Divine includes trust and belief, as well as focus or remembrance. As Jesus commented on feeling energy going out from Himself when a woman touched His robe in order to be healed, 'Your faith has made you whole.' When beings trust in divinity, divinity responds. Where there is no faith, divinity does not normally respond.

In this book, Irene describes the Shiva Lingams as being full of dark, convoluted energies that needed clearing and realigning. The lingams had been serving as collection points for darkness, but were not being cleared. Why was Shiva collecting the darkness, and why was the darkness not being cleared? Both Shiva and Shakti are fully Brahman, fully competent; both can, and on occasion do, perform any of the functions of the divine. In general, however, they voluntarily limit themselves to their assigned roles. So, Shiva also pulls darkness from Creation when He is asked. In this case, the Shiva Lingams were the focus and receptacles, and Shiva was the aspect of God being addressed. Darkness was being offered and accepted, but not being removed and replaced with Light.

Although Shiva could also have cleansed the lingams, He chose to permit the Mother to do so. But, as humans on Earth forgot about the Mother, or lost faith in Her, She ceased to clean these lingams. Even in India, one of the places where the Feminine Divine is still acknowledged and worshipped, the bulk of the faith and attention has turned, over the millennia, to the Masculine Divine. Of course, the Masculine Divine never dominated the Feminine, but on earth, this preference of humans was reflected by the divine. The lingams could have been cleared, but were left as examples of what happens when human beings lose faith.

With her visual metaphors of unblocking the Mother energy, Irene is heralding a coming turning-point in human evolution, when faith in the Mother will be restored on Earth. We are entering a time when the Mother and Father will both be worshipped, in balance, and in their proper, respective roles. Humans are reaching a point when they will understand the divine, and thereby come to reflect the divine on Earth.

Prof. Sue Evans
21.05.07

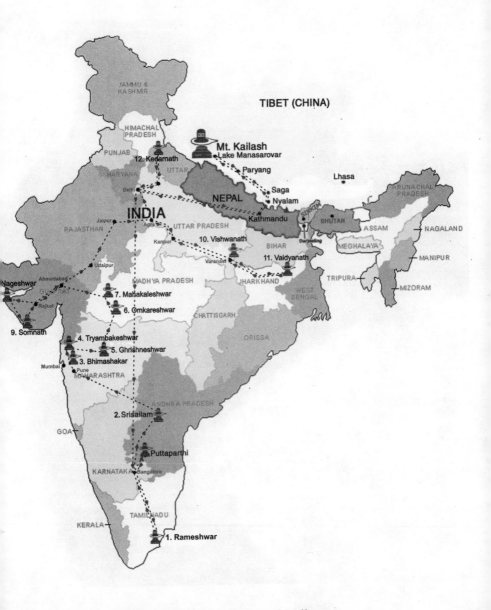

The 12 Jyotir Lingams of India

The Mt. Kailash – Manasarovar Yatra

THE 12 JYOTIR LINGAMS

06.06.06.
06.00 a.m.

BANGALORE.

Well, I don't know about another trip of a lifetime – but this I
know for sure – THIS IS THE TRIP OF MANY LIFETIMES!

A few months back I heard of the Shiva Temples – then more
specifically THE 12 JYOTIR LINGAMS!
On further enquiry, I found them to be scattered throughout India.
Stretching from the south – Rameshwaram, Tamil Nadu, to the
north – Mt. Kedarnath, Himalayas, the west – Nageshwar, near
Dwarka, Gujarat, and the east – Vaidyanath, Jharkhand / Bihar.

An interesting trip I thought, before realising they were in a
specific order 1-12. Then a further realization that they were
not in sequence.

After a period of adjustment with the Monkey Mind – Ego, I
surrendered to yet a far greater truth, and the realization this

1

was meant to be not only *my* journey, but a journey to help uplift the Human Spirit, by elevating the Energy, Frequency and Vibrations of Man, bringing about heightened Conscious Awareness and great and wondrous Planetary Change.

Lingam 1

RAMESHWAR
Rameshwaram, Tamilnadu

06.06.06.

LINGAM 1 – RAMESHWAR
Rameshwaram, Tamilnadu

The Rameshwar Lingam is situated at the southern most tip of India on the mountain Gandha Madhana, which is a very important pilgrimage site for Hindus.
Rameshwaram, according to legends, is the place where Lord Rama built a bridge across the sea to Lanka to rescue his consort Sita.

History suggests that Lord Rama established this sand Jyotir Lingam before winning the war with Ravana, the ruler of Lanka, after offering many prayers to Lord Shiva to grant boons to win the battle.
As Ravana, a son of Brahma had been killed in the battle – Rama sent Hanuman the Monkey God, to procure a Lingam from Shiva at Mt.Kailash. He returned to find the sand lingam already installed. Rama advised him to place the new Lingam beside the already installed one. This allowed 'both' to be worshipped.

3

Today I am at Rameshwaram – ready for tomorrow's expedition into the 'unknown'.

It was suggested that I begin working 90 kilometres from Rameshwaram, in a circular area, surrounding the first of my Shiva Lingams – Number 1 to me, but 9 in the normal sequence.

You ask – 'Why not begin at Lingam Number 1?'

Because I was told – South to West, East to North.

Upon delving a little deeper – I felt that this was an extremely practical way to see and experience the Shiva Lingams and Temples for my agenda, however NOT THE OPTIMUM way for the Spiritual Seeker!

THE INNER-VIEW:

What did I experience and see about 90 kilometres from Rameshwaram?

A huge – almighty golden Lingam. Smaller in size at first, then it expanded, the longer I kept looking – the normal Lingam shape above, however with a very pointed base. As I looked, it grew to encompass the whole 90 kilometre radius, and then the base grew and grew – reaching down into the Core of Mother Earth.

Down and yet further down it reached – searching – like it was looking for an anchor – the 'Yoni' – the feminine horizontal projection seen on many Lingams.

Prior to this, whilst it was still relatively small, about the size of the Temple, it had no real anchor. It appeared to be floating in the air, and *relatively* unstable.

A Vortex was then activated, and limitless amounts of dark energy were sucked up into the Vortex.

Only after the Lingam began shining in brilliance, did it begin to expand in width, height and depth.

Now back to the expansion – deeper and deeper still it went, searching for an anchor. Then out of Mother Earth came an anchor. The male part of the Lingam fitted into the anchor of Mother Earth – The Divine Feminine – Shakti.

4

Stabilization then took place – UNIVERSAL STABILIZATION. Varying amounts of energy were taken from two friends, Sue and Margot, during this time to help with the stabilization.

It was then I witnessed the Earth begin to move ever so gently, unlike before, when the darker energy was being removed. The energy required to help with the 'stabilization' was a horrific amount for a normal human being to provide. Fortunately Sue and Margot were *not* normal!

I could see Grid Lines and Graph Display Options. However, all the above groundwork – the Celestial Work – was to be completed the following day in the Temple itself.
It looked as though the energy of the Lingam had separated from Mother Earth, and since that time the land – energy had become very unstable in *that* particular area.

Whilst driving through Madurai I noticed a hotel advertisement for 'The Northgate Hotel' and then saw an advertisement for 'The City of Temples,' followed by a billboard reading 999. Then a little further on 33, 108, Royal Court, Fore Court, and many hammer and sickle pictures.

So dear Heavenly Father – do you have the energy to pass comment on the happenings of today?

Yes My Dear I do.
However first of all let us digress –
You must not drive more than 12 hours at one time; a maximum of 9 hours is preferable. You are not to drive after 6.30-7.00p.m. as you must be safely in your abode by then. You then are to shower, eat and write about your trip, The Journal of your travels. You are the 'boss' of this trip – not your driver or his co-driver.
Do you hear?

Otherwise they look around, eat and sleep, and you my dear will be still working. So no driving after 6.00 p.m. if at all possible – in readiness to facilitate work at 7.00 p.m.

Now regarding Sri Rama Lingeswaram.
It is a Lingam born out of Pride. NOT Ego but Pride!
Yes – Pride! Pride comes before a fall – and so it was.

This particular Lingam guards the Gateway to Lanka – the North Gate, with an Energy, Frequency and Vibration of 999, very rare indeed. It is highly symbolic, as it is Number 9 Lingam. Earlier it was encased in gold.
So see what tomorrow brings, and then write about it all.
You are too tired my sweet to write now.

07.06.06.
8.27 a.m.

Rameshwaram Temple – A Divine Blessing –
ANCHORING THE ENERGY OF THE MOTHER.

A little apprehensive I entered the huge, magnificent Temple, and was duly provided with a Tour Guide immediately.
First of all I bathed in the waters of the 22 Wells; finally arriving at the Jyotir Lingam, where Arathi took place.

Arathi: The waving of the Eternal Flame at the end of devotional singing – when you offer yourself to God, and reduce your cravings of the material world.

Blessings and yet more blessings, where I was guided to Goddess Parvathi.
The Divine Mother Earth Energy could be felt really deeply within the great walls of Rameshwaram. These walls were utilised for stabilization and gratification, of all of Humanity.

6

*Goddess Parvathi – The Divine Mother – Shakti – Devi –
are all aspects of the Feminine Form of Creation.*

Garlands of flowers were given in gratitude, and the most glorious
Lotus returned as prasadam. All in all an amazing experience.
Finally I walked past the 108 Shiva Lingams – praying and
chanting – 'Om Namaha Shivaya'.

**Yes the anchoring of The Divine Mother's Light, Love
and Energy.**
The tide will turn on Humanity NOW!
Her time WILL come!
**She will soon be free – for all the World to see – and bathe
in her Divine Bliss.**

**The Energy of North Gate – the Gate and Pathway to
Enlightenment for the betterment of Humanity –
OPENING THE NORTH GATE – AS IN OPENING THE
THIRD EYE – THE ONE.**

**Many thousands will weep as they bathe in the bliss in the
Sea of Lanka.**
**Chant the name of Rama 108 times – Om Sai Ram – all
will be on Earth, as it is in Heaven.**

Is the number 33 important?
**Yes, there are 33 Portals or 'Openings' to DISPEL the
Myths of the Illusion of Life.**

**Rameshwaram Temple was one of the finest architecture
wonders in its day. An absolute feat, and expounding the
virtue of LOVE – Great Love – the love Rama had for
Sita.**

The companionship and trust of Laxmana, the bearer of great gifts in the form of Hanuman, and Ganesha – Guardian of the Northern Gate.
However – Who is supreme?
Of course the mightiest of mighty – SHIVA – Lord Shiva – The ability to implode and explode the Myths of the COSMOS.

The MIGHTY Shiva – No-one is more powerful at this time on Earth than SHIVA – 'Lord of The Universe'.

All take note – the Mother Energy that has been blocked for Centuries has NOW been released as NEVER BEFORE!

All Portals of Transcendence will be opened for all to see and encapsulate – the wonders of the UNIVERSES!

Om Namaha SHIVAYA
Om Namaha SHIVAYA
Om Namaha SHIVAYA.

Glory to God in the Highest Form – The Form of the almighty Lord Shiva.
Om Om Om.

While driving along, after completing the visit to the Temple, I picked up the Lotus, and was guided to count the petals and to ask for the symbology – meaning, as a gesture of reverence and respect to The Divine Mother – Goddess Parvathi.

1. Love
2. Purity
3. Forgiveness
4. Excellence

5.   Gratitude
6.   Abundance
7.   Chivalry
8.   Mass Proportionate System
9.   Extraterrestrial Activity
10.   Subterranean thoughts / ideas / agendas for the highest good.
11.   Amalgamation of Truth
12.   Agendas governed and coveted by DIVINE WILL
13.   Anger
14.   Hate
15.   Obedience
16.   Germination of Love
17.   Distrust
18.   Mistrust
19.   Abuse of ALL Privileges
20.   Deeper Anger
21.   Resentment
22.   Humiliation
23.   1st Human Value – Truth
24.   2nd Human Value – Righteous Conduct
25.   3rd Human Value – Peace
26.   4th Human Value – Love
27.   5th Human Value – Non Violence – ALL 5 Values AS ONE
28.   Beauty – great inner beauty of
29.   Thoughts
30.   Words
31.   Deeds
32.   TO RESTORE BALANCE TO THE 3 WORLDS
33.   To DIMINISH The Shiva Energy
34.   To HEIGHTEN The Parvathi Energy
35.   THE POWER OF NOW
36.   Trust
37.   More Trust

38. Release of Instability
39. Forward thinking
40. PAST IS PAST
41. Cosmic Alignment
42. Futuristic Visions
43. Global deprivation of Liberty – THE EGO
44. Ascension
45. MASS CONSCIOUS AWARENESS
46. Planetary Change
47. Cosmic Consciousness
48. Dire needs
49. Control – extreme control
50. Heaviness of burdens
51. Steel / Iron – strength of character
52. Brass – determination
53. Copper – an insult
54. Silver – a majority
55. Gold – sublime
56. Paper – life giving through remnants
57. Cotton – purity, health, obedience
58. Service
59. Water
60. Air
61. Fire
62. Ether
63. Earth
64. Challenge
65. Righteousness
66. Who is Master – Who is Servant?
67. Solidity
68. Liquidity
69. Generate
70. Wealth
71. Abundance
72. Materialism

73. Royalty
74. Biblical Solution
75. King
76. Queen
77. God – ALL IS ONE
78. Goddess – ALL ASPECTS OF THE ONE
79. Lie
80. Manipulation
81. Deceit
82. Evil – Death of Ego
83. Injustice
84. Physical Death
85. Everlasting Life
86. God Centeredness
87. Oneness of Being
88. TRUTH – SATHYA
89. Companionship
90. Camaraderie
91. True Friendship
92. Limitless LOVE
93. True Abundance
94. Health
95. Wellbeing
96. A match made in Heaven
97. For YOU are The Kingdom – The Power and the Glory forever and ever. Amen.
98. BLESSINGS
99. Padnamaskar
100. Darshan
101. Patriation
102. Mother
103. Father
104. Son
105. Daughter
106. Child of God

107. LAMB OF GOD
108. God – Sathya – Truth
109. ALL GODS ARE ONE
110. Hindu
111. Buddhist
112. Christian
113. Moslem
114. Zorastrian
115. Cosmic Creation
116. Cosmic Cleansing
117. Completeness
118. The Four Winds of Chance and Change
119. Magic
120. Surrealism
121. Hope
122. Justice
123. Positive
124. Negative
125. Mirror
126. Image
127. Reflection
128. Removal of Obstacles – Big and small
129. Reincarnation
130. Travel
131. Horse
132. Donkey
133. Car
134. Train
135. Aeroplane
136. Motorcycle
137. Bicycle
138. Walk
139. Crawl
140. Roll
141. Sit

142. Stand
143. Elevation
144. Levitation
145. Calendar
146. Past Lives
147. Future Lives
148. PRESENT
149. Days
150. Minutes
151. Hours
152. Seconds
153. Night
154. Day
155. Hot
156. Cold
157. Peace
158. War
159. Sun
160. Moon
161. Hate
162. LOVE
163. Everlasting Glory
164. Flower
165. Bloom
166. Perfume
167. Stamen
168. Nectar
169. Sweetness
170. Liquid Honey
171. Amrit
172. Ashes to Ashes
173. Dust to Dust
174. Vibhuti
175. Sacredness
176. Nature

177. Green
178. Environment
179. Water
180. Snow
181. Ice
182. Extremely Cold
183. Skiing
184. Danger
185. Excitement
186. Exuberance
187. Heightened Awareness
188. BLISS – EVERLASTING + 108 Stamens

I find it impossible to believe one 'normal' looking Lotus can possibly explode into 188 Petals, not to mention the 108 Stamens.

Thinking about Rameshwaram and its great and wondrous ISOLATION.
A fishing village – an island of great beauty.

The Shiva Lingam – What is the significance of The Shiva Lingam?
To elevate Christ Consciousness and BALANCE the 3 Worlds by activation of the Feminine Aspect of God – The Divine Mother Energy.

Is the activation of all the 12 Jyotir Lingams after the energizing, to do with harnessing the Shiva Energy, then allowing it to FLOW forth in the Form of The Divine Feminine?

My dear, my dear – so many questions whilst you are driving.

The purest Form of Energy is that of the FEMININE, however first you have to cleanse, energize, expand and

proliferate – all Energies AS ONE, before they ALL become truly THE DIVINE FEMININE.
Then and only then, will your work be complete for Humanity AT THIS TIME!
All is as it should be.

The Shiva Lingam represents –
Explosion In Consciousness
Truth
Excellence
ALL IS ONE.

The RELEASE of The Divine God Energy to The Divine Goddess Energy, or release of The Masculine Energy to The Feminine Energy – THE OPENING UP OF A WELL OF LOVE.

Parvathi – The Jewel in The Crown of Shiva.
Representing the greatest Journey – The Mother Ganga.
Removing all sins of / from all Men – The Mother Ganga.
Purifying the Very Soul of Man – to allow for Cosmic Purification.
To bathe in The Mother is to bathe in BLISS.
Attainment of Absolution and Everlasting Glory – Moksha or Eternal Life!

08.06.06.
2.00 p.m.

The Journey – Yesterday and today have not been easy personality wise, with my driver. From the very first day there has been a problem. From my point of view, the trip for the driver seems to be all about control and 'who' is the boss!
Obviously the whole trip is karmic in transaction for the driver, his co-driver and myself, apart from the Lingam work. Although

15

on second thoughts – probably that is involved as well – All parts of THE ONE!

I guess it must be difficult for a driver to rely on what I say!
I *hear* the voice of God say do this and that – go here and there, and yet expect others to follow those particular instructions without too many questions. Some others cannot hear 'the voice' or see a form or vision.
So here I am suggesting we take a different route – more in line with the Shiva work, and yet the very thought of 'change' caused a *huge* upsurge in Negative Energy. Not directed at God, but directed at me – the personality aspect of Self.
After hearing God's voice I suggest this or that, however OTHERS ARE NOT READY TO HEAR THE TRUTH!
They only KNOW *their* truth, or the *supposed* truth!

So after MASSIVE Energetic discharge – being drenched in it, I have to remain in a state of EQUANIMITY! Unaffected by anger, fear, control, jealousy, frustration.
PATIENCE, EQUANIMITY AND MORE LOVE – IS MY AIM!
The stress has taken its toll, and erupted into a cold sore, and today spots are appearing all over my forehead – an allergy? To what? To whom?

Feeling a little better after having arrived back in Bangalore and then Whitefield, on the way through to our next destination. Tasty lunch and a brief chat with friends. So onwards and upwards! Stopped at a local pharmacy to collect some antihistamines. Written on the outside of the package in the most glorious colour was – FAITHFUL ASCENT!
THE MAHAMASTAKA ABHISHEKA – the giant spectacle of The Jains.

Interesting also was the fact that I had assumed Swami had long since left for Puttaparthi, and He was *still* at Brindavan.

I arrived – and *then* He left!
It was, as though He had been waiting for me – long enough to provide the extra stabilization I required, by altering my energy to continue the trip.
I asked if Swami wanted to talk with me now or later.

NOW – There is only THE PRESENT!
There is nothing else – PAST IS PAST.
Do not – I repeat, do not waste time or energy on thoughts or others' agendas or *supposed* wrong doings. Just bathe in the Bliss of The Divine.

I waited for you to arrive back – if you had been PRESENT, you could have seen me leave! But you were ABSORBED in THE PAST.
You have all experienced lessons these past few days.
Observe, but do not participate in others' agendas.

Where does the blame lie you ask?
There is NO blame!
ONE SHOULD NOT DEFLECT THE GLORY OF GOD!
You ALL pay the price for your own Transgressions.
You ask – surely not my co-driver? He is but an innocent young boy! Yes surely – But 'Who' has he been in Past Lives? Who are YOU to say innocent?
I alone am the judge of others – I PASS JUDGEMENT – not you or your senior driver.

What was the real problem?
A battle of Wills and Ego. Both of you were working from your head – NOT FROM YOUR HEART!
Remember – the mainstay of Life IS LOVE!
Nothing more – nothing less.
Release ALL back to me now; seek forgiveness to, and from others, and all will once again flow in, and with the Divine Nectar of Light and Love.

You *think* bad thoughts –
You *do* bad things –
THEN YOU BOTH WILL SUFFER THE
CONSEQUENCES!
And mark my word – they are consequences you will not
want to have placed on your path – at this stage of your
journey.
Forgive your driver, and send him MORE LOVE.

Om Sai Ram
Om Namaha Shivaya
Om Shanti Shanti Om.

Take rest now sweet One for one hour.
I am Lord of THE UNIVERSE.
Remember the lady from the phone company, and her
grace!

SRISAILAM / MALLIKARJUNA
Srisailam, Andhra Pradesh

09.06.06.

LINGAM 2 – SRISAILAM
Srisailam, Andhra Pradesh

When Kumar Kartikeya returned to Kailash after completing his trip around the earth, he heard about His brother Ganesha's marriage from Narada. This angered him greatly so he left for Krounch mountain. Lord Shiva and Parvathi searched for him, but he kept moving further away. They decided to leave a light on every mountain they visited for their son.
It is believed Shiva and Parvathi visit this place on Amavasya (no Moon day) and Pournami (full Moon day) respectively.

Lord Shiva was extremely pleased with the devotion of the demon Gajasura, and granted him darshan with Parvathi. The demon praised the Divine couple, and as a boon sought that they be manifest in Lingam Form.

Visiting this Jyotir Lingam not only blesses one with innumerable wealth, but also fame, and fulfils desires.

An exhausting day! Interesting, however quite exhausting.

We left Bangalore early – 5.30 a.m. with an expectation to arrive at Srisailam to see the Jyotir Lingam, then travel yet further onwards to rest for the night, before exploring another part of India. The trip took four and a half hours, and the same amount of time to find a hotel for the night.

Srisailam is situated on the banks of the River Krishna.

On the south bank of the river lies the massive Fort, enclosed with six feet high walls. The Temple was not what I had anticipated – so I looked at 'expectations and outcomes' again! The landscape beautiful, not unlike Kodaikanal in the south of India – green and mountainous – an old Hill Station – left over from the days of 'The Raj'.

Joined with the thronging masses, eventually coming face to face with the actual Lingam. Earlier I had bought a half coconut in the form of prasadam from a Priest.

It was difficult to see the 'actual' Lingam as it was covered in garlands of flowers, so I gently placed the half coconut on top of the Lingam. The Priests nearly had a fit!

I continued to pray and give thanks.

Finally I arrived at the Sri Rajarajeshwari Devi Statue, where yet more prayers and arathi were offered to Amma, the Divine Mother.

The Temple is situated hundreds of feet higher than the river, so the two drivers and I caught a cable car down to the water's edge, where more prasadam was offered to the river, in the form of flowers. The catchment area of the river is not unlike the magnificence of the Hoover Dam in America, however on a smaller scale.

THE INNER – VIEW:

I could see two golden inverted triangular pyramids, spanning about 10 metres from the core of the Temple. The apex of the two pyramids gently balancing on each other. The energy very light and delicate – unlike in every way to the energy of Rameshwaram.

Then as I watched, I could see dark swirls or coils of old energy, so removed all of that. It flowed from deep in the centre of the pyramid.

Originally the pyramids were not attached at the apex, but at the solid base. It was only after 'the clearing' that they spun around and inverted – point to point. Then I was told the apex energy was Shiva Energy, and the base energy was Mother Energy.

It was as though the Shiva Energy had to be dispersed or lessened, to *allow* the Mother Energy to blossom forth and become very powerful.

Pull down the Shiva Energy into the Womb of The Mother!

As I kept looking, the apex of the two pyramids began to slide into each other – forming a diamond, but only to the centre of each individual pyramid. The tip / apex of the Shiva Pyramid seemed to be still searching, so even further down it went deep into the core of Mother Earth, looking for yet another anchor.

Eventually the shapes began to form 'The Star of David,' and the most brilliant light – not only light, but light in density.

It was then I heard – UNLEASHING THE POWER OF THE MOTHER, and knew it was not only referring to Mother Earth, but also The Divine Mother of all Mothers.

My own energy felt a little scattered here, as opposed to Rameshwaram, where it was extremely concentrated and focused.

Yes my dear – too much 'thinking' and not enough 'listening' to your inner God Self.

You arrived in an already weakened state spiritually.

Irene – I do not think you still understand the magnitude

of THIS Work! There is no room *for* mistakes. You must be 100% focused, and be led here and there by me – not by your driver – either one of them. You must partake of THIS adventure ALONE. Only then will you hear my voice, not the voices of others and their agendas!

I need for you to be clear! If you had been – you would have seen a totally different picture to what you have just described. It would have been yet more complex and interesting!

First of all the energy was 180 kms. outwards from the Temple as you *first* thought. Yes, you saw the golden Pyramid and reflection beneath. This was what you first saw! A mirror reflection – Shiva Energy on the top, and The Mother Energy below.

As you began to remove the negative energy, you began to see the negative coil of darkness only on the 'top' of the Pyramid NOT below! It was 'blocked' Shiva Energy.

For millions of years – the Male Energy has dominated The Mother, however NOW is the time for great and wondrous RELEASE.

The Pyramids inverted and then converted to form The Star of David. However only after the 'tip' of the Shiva Pyramid had penetrated through to the Womb of The Mother.

It was then it was looking for its anchor – and the anchor was found.

Another anchor and 'another' Lingam, being utilised as a BASE ANCHOR.

So two Temples and two anchors to clear the old Shiva blocked energy, and release the clear, true energy of and from The Mother.

Om Namaha Shivaya
Om Namaha Shivaya
Om Shanti Om.

A Trilogy of Blessings were given Globally today –
The Divine Mother
The Divine Father
The Divine Child.

Om Sai Ram.

10.10.06.

Since the visit to Rameshwaram, many small blisters have erupted on my forehead.

Today I thought to ring Margot, she suggested I stop taking one of the 'Vibrational Medicines' Swami has said to take, so we will see the outcome!

I feel it may all be related to the stress of the trip.
What stress you ask?
The trip has not been easy in many ways, and yes I know it is activating my personality flaws!
However the driving for 12–15 hours daily! Some instances, not to mention yesterday – 12 hours to cover 300kms – rough and narrow roads – full of the unexpected!

Also, energetically it is amazing to observe the energies of my two drivers! All seems to have settled now – so long as I do what I am told!
So whose trip is this?
You may well ask!
God's Trip – My trip – My drivers thought differently!

23

Hopefully NOW we are on THE SAME PAGE of the book! The minute there appeared to be a slight deviation from Swami's original plans – then literally ALL HELL BROKE LOOSE!

Release Control,
Release all thoughts of Self,
Release the trapped love from your heart – EMBRACE ALL, for all the World to see, hear, know and EXPERIENCE!

Om Sai Ram
Om Namaha Shivaya
Om Shanti Om.

Lingam 3

BHIMASHANKAR
Dakini, Maharashtra

12.06.06.

LINGAM 3 – BHIMASHANKAR.
Dakini, Maharashra.

There are three thoughts as to the location of this particular Lingam, and it is this location that I was guided to visit.

The story is told that the father of Bhima was killed by Rama, and Bhima developed great hatred towards him. After meditating on Brahma to give him strength, his ego increased dramatically, and he conquered the Worlds. The people in all the Worlds prayed to Lord Shiva, who agreed to kill the demon Bhima, and reduce him to ashes.
It was then Shiva agreed to install himself in Lingam Form as Bhimashankar.

A few days rest in Pune; now we are on the way to Bhimashankar Jyotir Lingam.
Personally I'm feeling more rested after a gruelling 17 hour trip from Kurnool to Pune. Yesterday I just could not get out of bed, no work of any description in a Spiritual sense. Well maybe a

little, however now I am feeling much stronger and more settled.
Occasionally still dealing with a few feelings and emotions of
abandonment, ego, control, frustration and arrogance.
Mine – you ask?
Well if in fact I mirror others – then I guess the answer is YES!

THE INNER-VIEW:
What did I see when 'tuning in' to the next Lingam from a distance
of 90 kms?
A golden Circle containing a golden Pyramid, however 'inside'
the Pyramid the energy was really dark / black – NEGATIVE.
It has been trapped for thousands of years.
The Circle is set on an axis as well – with poles extending above
and below.

Drink 'more' water before you arrive to do the work!

The scenery – much like the Yarlung Valley in Tibet and the
area around Milarepa's Cave.
Four-wheel drive vehicles are obviously a better option for travel
here if possible. About half way along the winding road we saw
a huge reservoir of water – a huge dam.
Is this the Bhima River in the valley?
Nuts are being grown here, on the roof of the world.

Finally a sighting of Bhimashankar.
It is a beautiful intricately carved Temple, constructed by the
eminent Nana Phadnavis, which houses this Jyotir Lingam –
with Nandi, the bull – The Vehicle of Lord Shiva.

First I knelt and showered the Lingam with leaves and flowers.
Resting yet once again my hands – first right and then left – on
the actual Lingam, in situ on the floor of the Temple. This was
followed by an 'offering' from the Priests.

Once we were outside, I formalised my commitment to 'Our Lord,' by bathing my feet in the spring as well.

Whilst looking over the water – a vortex opened, and the dark energy from the 'top' section of the Pyramid was sucked into the vortex. The darker energy from the 'base' section was sucked back into Mother Earth.

Conception of The Energy of The Divine Mother.

An explosion of light from the middle of the Pyramid occurred. Then the whole circle, pyramid and axial poles, filled with light. Then the poles began to rotate and spin really quickly, and yet *more* gold light was expelled. Then the axial pole became 'The Trident' of Lord Shiva!

This experience allowed The Divine Energy to maximize its full potential, as all began to balance and harmonize.

It was a truly amazing experience.

Baba – do you have any comments?

Yes my dear I do!

The Negative Aspect of Human Existence has been rightfully restored to its normal balance.

The Durga Energy will NOW reign supreme here.

This will NOW become a Temple of Healing – NOT a Temple of Transition – yet once again. All who touch this particular Lingam will have 'The Blessing' of Durga, to help *ease* their path to Moksha / Enlightenment.

Yet once again – The Divine Mother Energy WILL REIGN SUPREME.

You ask – 'But Swami, they are all Shiva Lingams. Where is the Shiva Jyotir Lingam Energy?'

For the UPLIFTMENT of Humanity at this time – The Mother Earth Energy will reign SUPREME, in whatever FORM I deem it to be.

Om Namaha Shivaya
Om Om Om.

Whilst travelling down the mountain we experienced a heavy shower of rain.

Cleansing and Healing by The Mother has NOW begun in earnest.

Om Shanti Om.

TRYAMBAKESHWAR
Nasik, Maharashtra

13.06.06.
9.30 a.m.

LINGAM 4 – TRYAMBAKESHWAR.
Nasik, Maharashtra.

The Divine sage Gautama and wife Ahalya lived a pious life with pure intent. However they lived in the midst of others of jealous behaviour, who prayed to Lord Ganesha to banish them from their ashram. After much counselling Ganesha could not change their mind so agreed. Ganesha appeared in the ashram garden as an ill looking cow.
Gautama threatened the cow with a blade of grass and the cow died.
The other sages asked Gautama and Ahalya to leave as they had killed a 'sacred' Cow.
The others were still not satisfied, so asked Gautama to go around the Brahmagiri mountain many times performing Divine Mantras, and then meditate on Lord Shiva to atone for his sins.
Shiva was very pleased and granted the couple liberation,

after explaining the jealous actions of the others. The couple asked for the other sages to be forgiven.
Lord Shiva granted their wish and stayed in Tryambakeshwar with the Divine Mother.

Last evening was spent in Nasik, where I stayed at the Taj Hotel. Joy, oh joy for true abundance. What some take as their due or normal – I thank God one hundred times for the comfort, great food, ambience, and general overall helpfulness of and from the staff.

We are on our way to the Temple, it is about 30 kilometres east of Nasik.
All I see at the moment is a circle of Eagles in Spirit Form, with huge wing spans of 6-8 feet across, emerging from the three Lingam holes, increasing in size as they reach the sky.
Many Northern American Indians are coming into my vision now. This area has the highest amount of Extra-terrestrial (ET) Energy at *this* time, in regard to the 12 Jyotir Lingams.

Yes my dear so it has, and so it will always be.
This area – the whole 30 kilometre range, including the town of Nasik, has borderline Negative ET influences and Cosmic Trends. The energy here has become yet once again congested, however this time by Cosmic Trends and Influences.

As the Global Awareness increases, the energies, frequencies and vibrations (EFV) alter accordingly – trying to align themselves with the Universal Energies.
However, the 'normal' Human Element is still incapable of TRUE change at this time, because of let us say Cosmic or Universal Interference.

Fear, great fear of the future, has created this timely dilemma.

Just realign ALL energies for the highest good as ONE. Don't forget to remove any or ALL obstructions first though, and please PROTECT yourself here!

Om Sai Ram.

Now back to the Lingam.

First of all we lined up to gain access into the main Temple area. There were many Priests performing Puja with selected families in the centre area, which was cordoned off. Chanting and prayers were being sung aloud.

The square white marbled area was exactly beneath a huge domed ceiling – all of the stonework appeared old and darkened with age.

A large mirror had been erected on an angle, so one could see the 3 Lingams embedded in the floor.

At this particular time the Lingams were being cleansed, so we all stood back and waited for the ritual to be completed by the Priests.

I felt a little sad at first that they were being cleansed, and then realised it was a highly 'symbolic' gesture, and most probably not performed many times a day.

A HIGHLY RITUALISATION SYMBOL OF GOD'S TRUTH!

After 'the viewing,' the Priest suggested I sit in the middle of the Temple under the dome, for a meditation.

THE INNER-VIEW

Amazing – Shiva came in with true empowerment and strength, and with Trident in his hand.

Shiva stood at the outer edge of the 3 Lingams and pierced the ground with his Trident, moving it around to enlarge the hole.

Trident: A three pronged Spear

He tapped the Lingams in order, beginning from the left side.

1ˢᵗ Tapping:
Lingam 1 – 4 taps. Lingam 2 – 8 taps. Lingam 3 – 12 taps.
Then once again he placed the Trident into the centre of the each Lingam, and began to enlarge the orifice – quite aggressively.

2ⁿᵈ Tapping:
Lingam 1 – 2 taps. Lingam 2 – 6 taps. Lingam 3 – 13 taps.
Followed by another enlargement of the hole, and then a breakthrough to Mother Earth.

3ʳᵈ Tapping:
Lingam 1 – 3 taps. Lingam 2 – 6 taps. Lingam 3 – 9 taps.
This was to bring into alignment and harmony ALL Energies of the 3 Worlds – AS IS ABOVE IS BELOW.

The Three Worlds – the Subterranean or underground Worlds back to the Core of Existence; the Earth and Universe, as we know it to be; and the Heavens above – the Gateway to the Stars and the many Universes we are yet to encounter in our physical experience.

With the 'clearing' of the 3 Lingams, the Negative Energy was literally sucked back into Mother Earth. It was akin to 'The washing away of the Sins of Humanity,' and the other levels of Consciousness and Form.

Finally one last piercing of the Earth by Shiva's Trident, and the golden light from The Mother encompassed the 3 Lingams, and they began to illuminate internally – pure gold.

Whilst meditating I had also asked for the Temple area to be cleared from Negative ET / Cosmic / Universal Energies as ONE.

Some energy was sucked upwards into the Vortex, however predominantly the larger proportion was washed into the Earth.

Yes my dear – Healing the Wounds of ALL Mankind on your Planet, and the other Beings on other Planets as well.

These 3 Lingams – The Tryambakeshwar Lingams, are very important in their individual right, as well as collectively.

They represent the Deities of Vishnu, Saraswati and Laxshmi collectively.
Vishnu – Lord of the Universe.
Saraswati – Goddess of Knowledge.
Laxshmi – Goddess of Wealth.

You ask – 'Is not Parvathi involved?'
Are not you the inquisitive one Irene?

All Goddesses are representative of The Divine Aspect of ALL Creation. They become ONE with the Universal Energies, to bring balanced Harmony to the 3 Worlds.
So in a deeper sense – Who is the activator of Mother Earth?
It is none other than The Divine Aspect of Me –
My Shakti – as I am in *this* Form on Earth.
So I am ALL – I am Shiva / Shakti.
It is I who activate all in whichever Form I deem them to be.

I AM ONE WITH THE UNIVERSAL INTENTION FOR THE GOOD AND UPLIFTMENT OF HUMANITY ON EARTH, AND OTHER FORMS OF BEINGS IN OTHER UNIVERSES.

The Energy of The Tryambakeshwar Jyotir Lingams are NOW cleansing your Earth and Man, from depravation and sin.

ONLY LOVE WILL ILLUMINATE THE VERY SOUL OF MAN.

All who see these 3 Lingams as ONE – will bathe in the bliss of Rama.
Chant the name of Rama, and the hearts of Men will open spontaneously, allowing THE LOVE TO FLOW YET ONCE AGAIN.

Om Sai Ram.

12.03 p.m.

Thinking about Shiva and Parvathi, then I saw Shiva piercing the Earth, and he was thinking of her.

She is a part of me, and never far from my thoughts.
The Negative Energy will drain into the womb of The Mother.
I PIERCE THE MOTHER WITH LOVE OF PARVATHI.

Driving and observing the scenery – beautiful valleys surrounded by huge tablelands.
While in the car we are listening to Swamis' students chanting the Vedas with English translations – an excellent idea and far more interesting for the average Westerner.

Lingam 5

GRISHNESHWAR
Daulatabad, Maharashtra

13.06.06

LINGAM 5 – GRISHNESHWAR.
Daulatabad, Maharashtra.

A deeply religious Brahmin, Sudhamudu and wife Sudheha could not have children, so Sudheha asked her sister Ghrusma Devi to marry her husband to give him a child. Ghrusma Devi was truly devoted to Lord Shiva, and had immersed in a water tank 100 lingams she had made from earth and sand.
As the son grew and married, the first wife began to feel jealousy and hatred towards her sister. One day in a rage she killed the son, and threw his body in to the water tank with the lingams.
As the mother continued praying and doing puja to the lingams, she saw her son come out of the water. Lord Shiva appeared and blessed them both. The son threatened to seek revenge on his mother's sister, but his mother appealed to Lord Shiva to shower his grace upon the sister. He granted her wishes and transformed himself into the Grishneshwar Lingam.

Another view is that it was Parvathi who created this Lingam by the friction of her thumb. So she called the Lingam Grishneshwar – meaning friction.

Driving along towards Aurangabad, then quite unexpectedly saw the next Jyotir Lingam sign.

Do I go now or later?

Then Swami said 'Do not attempt to visit anymore than ONE Jyotir Lingam per day'.

Encountered a little pressure from the drivers to go, as it was only 8 kilometres from the highway – otherwise another 2-3 hour trip tomorrow to backtrack. So briefly thought about The Grishneshwar Lingam, and decided to call in – but against my better judgement energetically!

Amazing – absolutely glorious!

The entrance to the Temple area was through a small opening about 3 feet high. The whole Temple was made from small red bricks, with intrinsically carved pillars and stones. It was the most *intimate* Temple yet!

There on the floor, surrounded by Priests and devotees of Lord Shiva, was the Lingam.

Flowers were placed on the top and base of the Lingam, and then coconuts and money were placed on the outer rim. A copper chalice hung from above, dripping water onto the Lingam.

As I stood there in awe, the Lingam was freed and cleansed from others' flowers, and then milk was poured over the top, and all began washing it. I placed my flowers on the top of the Lingam, and then a beautiful Soul gave me a container of water to dribble over the Lingam as well.

As I knelt and touched the base – the emotions began to flow, and then as I touched the Lingam again, still more emotions!

The energy was *so* loving! I can hardly begin to describe the feeling. Then my forehead touched the base, middle and top of the Lingam.
All was blissful FOR JUST A MOMENT IN TIME!

In the courtyard of The Temple, was 'The Trident' Shiva used to pierce the ground for Parvathi – to access water from the Netherworld.
Parvathi first saw great light emanating from this area when she was grinding the vermilion and saffron powder for the centre parting of her hair.

On the way again, and driving past the most glorious Fort.
A Fort sitting on top of a pyramid of stone, covered by masses of greenery. Apparently the Fort was built in the Moghul Empire. At the present we are driving around the base – it is huge, resplendent, awesome, overpowering.

The experience before reaching this Jyotir Lingam – none.
Was it because I had attempted to work with two different energies on the one day? Then I remembered what Swami had said – 'Only one Lingam at the most per day!'
Now Swami says He will explain to me exactly what I missed! Another lesson for me I guess, as my first instinct was not to see or be in the energy of two Lingams in one day.

Yes my dear – yet another lesson for you.
Expanding on and around the Temple area and outwards to an area of 30 meters approximately, was a dense underground concentration of sulphur. This was activated by deep and intense volcanic pressures, brought about by Earth changes in the Subterranean levels of strata – or The Earth Layers.

The energy was blocked and quite poisonous, if consumed in large doses. Fortunately this was rarely the case, as

there are many outlets for pressure release in this particular area.
The pressure release areas extend for 30 kilometres from the actual Lingam.

If you look now as you drive, you will observe many variations in the landscape around here. This is mainly due to the Earth's pressure release systems being activated. And yes, what did you notice just a few moments ago? Yes, yes, the odour of Sulphur.

By clearing the 'centre' area of the Jyotirlinga – the convoluted and stagnated energy from the circle 30 metres to 30 kilometres in diameter, began to flood into the Earth, draining back into Mother Earth. This of course will destabilize the pressures yet once again.
However, now the Shiva Light of Love and Potency will flow forth into Mother Earth – and in return the Mother will assimilate ALL pressure changes into The Divine Well of Light and Love.

Om Sai Ram.

You ask 'How can Light and Love change the Sulphur content or Pressure Release Mechanisms of The Earth?'

Do none of you listen?

THERE IS ONLY ONE TRUTH FOR HUMANITY AND THAT TRUTH IS LOVE.
God's Truth is ONE.
The vibration of Love alone will alter and change The Tide of Humanity!
ONLY LOVE WILL SET YOU ALL FREE!

OMKARESHWAR
East Nimar, Madhya Pradesh

14.06.06.

LINGAM 6 – OMKARESHWAR
East Nimar, Madhya Pradesh.

Omkareshwar Lingam is the merging of the Omkareshwar and Amareshwar Lingams, which were located on the south and north of the mountain.
Vindhya prayed and meditated to Lord Shiva to enable him to stay with his consort on the mountain. Shiva appeared and blessed him, and merged the two lingams.

In the ancient times the Demons defeated the Gods or Divines. Indra was worried. The Demons created havoc in the 3 Worlds. In order to empower the Divines once again, Lord Shiva assumed the form of Jyotirmaya Omkaroop. The Gods worshipped the Lingam, which made them powerful once again.

Thinking about Swami, the Shiva Work and the Lingams.
Apparently a few days ago, Swami became really strong.

He actually walked to a *normal* car, and gave Darshan. However yesterday he was back to looking frail, and utilising the wheel chair again.

The one thing I have not been doing, is asking Swami daily how this Shiva work is affecting his HUMAN FORM at the moment.

Yes my dear, you have been VERY remiss!
You think – Monkey Mind / Ego, your daily trip ends with REST!
WRONG!
Your daily adventure is complete only after you speak with me!
So 5 Jyotir Lingams and you missed asking how Swami was feeling? You look into My Eyes and see Baba, and yet you see Shiva at the Jyotir Lingams.
For the last time – I AM ALL!

The Omkareshwar Lingam within the Temple is situated on an Island shaped like an 'Om' – the holiest of all Hindu Symbols.
The island is one mile long and half a mile wide, and at the junction of the Narmada and Kaveri Rivers.

THE INNER-VIEW:
The energy was dark, dark, the dark, deep, spiritual waters of hell for some, and the Gateway to The Netherworlds for others.
A Golden Crucifix hung in the air, however covering the darkness inside.
'Fool's Gold,' Swami just said.

This particular Lingam spreads the Negative Energy for 30 kilometres from the Jyotir Lingam. The Energy is a mix of the ancient Tribes, and their negative Tribal Systems.
The Systems stating – Who is King? Who is Master? Who is Servant? Who is Slave?
Ego reigned supreme in the earlier times, then through the

placement of The Lingam the energy cleared, and for a period of time, balanced the Earth and rudimentary chakras. However this period of time was short lived, and Ego – The Root of ALL Evil, reared its ugly head again.

By Shiva touching the Jyotir Lingam NOW, or The Lord's Energy resting upon the Lingam NOW – the energy released will automatically clear the darker energy from the underbelly or underside of the Crucifix.
Then once again – LIGHT AND LOVE WILL REIGN SUPREME!

The landscape driving towards Omkareshwar was wondrous and amazing. Plateaus of desert as far as the eye could see – surrounded by steep hills and winding roads.
On nearing Omkareshwar – the scenery changed to one of a more green and bush / tree variety.
Finally just on dusk, and after a 15 hour drive, we arrived in the village.

Down, down the steps of the village, through great and wondrous lanes, eventually reaching a walking path.
Finally across the mighty river to visit the Temple.
The view from the bridge was spectacular – just as the literature had described. Terrace upon terrace, covered with the most unbelievable architecture. Buildings of every shape and size, however all seeming to blend together as ONE.

High on the Island stood the Omkareshwaram Temple in all its glory. However downwards, downwards, through more winding lanes to near the water's edge, and the entrance to the actual Temple and Lingam. More queues yet once again, fortunately not as long as usual, due to the lateness I assume. After the usual *trying* moments – The Lingam!

I bent over and gently placed my 'offering' – a garland of flowers on to the top of the Lingam.

'Om Namaha Shivaya,' it called to me, although apparently I did not hear it, Swami said.

A Priest blessed me and gave me some prasadam (blessed food), and after praying I left to observe the beauty of the Temple.

Unfortunately it was surrounded by many Priests of all descriptions – many asking 'Do you want Puja,' so a rather harrowing experience, as money would then have changed hands.

My guide was a wonderful protector.

How would a mature Western Woman manage alone?

Not very well at many of these Temples!

English is very limited, and most signage is written in the language or dialect of that particular State. Even whilst driving most signs were NOT in English!

THE INNER-VIEW:

Now back to Omkareshwar Lingam.

First of all there was a Circle surrounding a Triangle / Pyramid, with a golden Crucifix inside.

As I touched the Lingam and prayed to God for salvation for all Humanity, the Negative Energy from the Crucifix expelled and entered the enclosed area of the Triangle / Pyramid.

The Triangle inverted, and then slid downwards, until the Apex was resting on the Lingam. The Negative Energy then drained into the Mother – Mother Earth.

Eventually all was glorious and wonderful, as a huge Golden Star 'exploded' forth, and the energy TRANSFORMED the Earth.

The light went straight upwards through the Apex of the Triangle or Pyramid into the Crucifix, and expanded outwards to the circumference of the Circle.

The Energy here – in past times MISSAPPROPRIATED the changes in the DNA Patterning. In other words prevented or limited the Spiritual growth of some Spiritual Aspirants.

Vast amounts of stagnated Kali Energies were removed, and the balance to the 3 Worlds restored.
All in all a very beautiful experience.
As the days progress the energy will expand outwards from here, and flow forth to help with the upliftment of Humanity.

Yes my dear – The rich get richer and the poor remain poor!
All is not well in the Realm of the Spiritual Aspirant.
Those who seek wealth, fame and fortune, will compromise their Spiritual Growth, unless they too will help heal the rift between rich and poor. To help bring into effect – the natural balance of the Earth, and all who live there at this time.

All of this Lingam work is about only one thing –
TO BRING BACK THE DIVINITY TO THE MOTHER –
ALL MOTHERS.

But all Mothers have Divinity you ask?
Yes, yes, I am talking about the Divinity from outside you all know to be.
Be it God, Buddha, Allah, Rama, The Messiah – To the God within.

When you are ALL in alignment for 'The' Highest Good – not 'Your' Highest Good, then that pure Form of Divinity, LOVE – will flow on to the rest of Humanity AS ONE.
Only when *this* occurs WILL THE ENERGY OF DIVINTY OR LOVE – TRANSFORM THE EARTH.

Yesterday you unblocked and unlocked A SEQUENTIAL TIME FLOW, to allow the Energy of The Mother to burst forth in all her glory – Glory to God.

The DNA Patterning and Activation you are so concerned about will alter dramatically now.
NOW is the time for true change.
As before – the Energy of Love will illuminate Mankind.

All of the Lingams activated thus far have already expanded their energy 100 fold; however this energy will not manifest as PURE LIFELINE DIVINITY until you tie the Energy of ALL Lingams together as ONE – and then walk around Mt. Kailash.
Then and only then will you be able to see the overall Bigger Picture, and then know what to activate and when.
Yes my dear, it is as you thought. An activation of The Light to help illuminate those Souls – both Light and Dark, and help them pass through into everlasting bliss.

Please remain focused and awake today, as Darker Energies are around your Light, all wanting just one thing – TO SAVE THEMSELVES.
Please illuminate their Souls before you begin your journey today.

Om Sai Ram.

'The Mother' you ask?
Yes, the Kali Energy eons ago was supreme.
Now it has been transformed into the Energy of balance / harmony / truth / peace / righteous conduct / non-violence, and most importantly of ALL – LOVE.
All is as it should be.
Blessings in the Name of The Father.

I activated The Light, and all of the Dark Beings around me, were sucked up into a Vortex of Light.

Wrong Irene, look closer. The real danger was closer to you!
Good – yes, your driver and co-driver needed clearing. You must remember to clear them both religiously, not to mention your car, whilst attending to other work!

Lingam 7

MAHAKALESHWAR
Ujjain, Madhya Pradesh

15.06.06.

LINGAM 7 – MAHAKALESHWAR.
Ujjain, Madhya Pradesh.

The main deity Shiva in the Lingam Form is believed to be Swayambhu (born of itself), deriving currents of power (Shakti) from within itself, as against the other lingams which are ritually established and invested with Mantra-Shakti.

The king and peoples of the Ujjain Kingdom prayed with total devotion to Lord Shiva.
A five year old boy witnessed the ritual and began to pray and perform puja every day to a small stone. His mother called him, but the small boy refused to move. The mother became angry and threw the stone away. The boy fell down exhausted and weeping. Shiva heard the small boy's prayers, and erected a beautiful temple to house this most glorious lingam. News of the manifestation spread throughout the Kingdom, and all recognized the boy to be a great soul.

Ujjain was purportedly the Greenwich of old.
Could this be the reason for the naming of this particular Lingam?
Maha – Great
Kal – Time
Eshwar – God.

THE INNER-VIEW:
Travelling towards the next Jyotir Lingam.
Is there no light around these areas, or should I say – no TRUE Light!
From an area of 44 kilometres in circumference there is a dark Circle with a Diamond coming forth from the base.
The upper portion of the diamond also encapsulated in darkness.
The lower portion embraced in light, and extending towards the Temple, and more importantly, the Jyotir Lingam itself.

This Lingam, and yesterday's Lingam – Omkareshwar, are linked by a faint horizontal energy line.
After the unblocking and unlocking of the energy today, the line will become dense and extremely concentrated. It appears that is all, however The Lord is saying – 'Wait and see – You are in TRUE Shiva Territory now'!

Upon touching the Lingam, the Shiva Energy became heightened, and the pure and loving energy from The Mother, flowed upwards into the darker areas of the diamond, and into the circle.
Then the energy travel outwards along the energy line – connecting the Mahakaleshwar Lingam to Omkareshwar Lingam.
The energy from Omkareshwar Lingam *appeared* to have stopped half way along the faint energetic line.

The energy from Mahakaleshwar Lingam travelled at a higher speed towards the other energy. At exactly half way they met and the energy erupted into a huge explosion – A COSMIC DANCE!

It was as though the energy from 'both' Lingams intensified many fold, into the *most* extraordinary brilliance at the ONE time.

Om Namaha Shivaya

What an experience – what a glorious sight to behold.
'Simultaneous Explosions of Shiva Energy,' to embrace Cosmic Alignment, Harmony and Peace.

Here we have 'Om' – the sound or vibration manifested as the land MASS shape / space at Omkareshwar, directly energetically linked by light with time at Mahakaleshwar. Einstein's Equation: $E = MC^2$

Cosmic Dance: Fritjof Capra, Author of 'Tao of Physics' and others as well, equates with the patterns created by subatomic particles in each atom. In other words – ALL IS ONE.

Yes my dear, this is so – and so it will be.
You will all be held accountable for the sins of the flesh of Man.
You waste Time, Energy and Money – but it is not only these 3 Elements you are wasting – IT IS LIFE YOU ARE WASTING!

You came, you saw, you acknowledged with reservation, the Truth of Sri Sathya Sai Baba – and waited yet for another reunion with God – maybe elsewhere?
Do not you all understand as yet – I AM ALL!
This I have explained many times over and over again. Do you all listen?
Some do, few do – some do not understand as yet.

I came to save Humanity in Human Form, not just as a Human Guru from which you take – and give NOTHING in return!
I GIVE – YOU GIVE – THIS IS THE LAW!
The law you must ALL accept, and then God Realization will be yours in this lifetime here on Earth.

The Shiva Energy today was unblocked by a Mother from THE MOTHER.
The Feminine Energy of ALL Creation about to burst forth, and yet once again – illuminate the World.
Peace, Peace, Peace, be with you all.
Accept what I came to give, however then give what it is you have received.
In the name of The Lord – Shiva, Sathya, Shirdi – ALL IS ONE.

Om Namaha Shivaya.

Well – here I am sitting at breakfast after the Lingam visit.
What can I say?
Glorious, supreme – amazing yet once again!

First of all the mandatory baskets of flowers, sweets, coconuts were gathered for the Puja, and then I entered the Temple area.
What a Divine Blessing was in store!
I had previously asked Baba for some *special* acknowledgement or sighting as to 'Who' He really is! It's not that I don't believe Swami IS ALL SUPREME – but every now and then I love to see the Physical Proof!

The Lingam was not open to the public, as the Priests were cleansing it for the morning ritual – a blessing in itself!
It was huge, about 2-3 feet tall – the largest Lingam yet.

I stood and watched as it was cleansed with milk, decorated with vermilion, garlanded with flowers, followed by Arathi.

There I was totally immersed and engrossed in the experience, when three bells began to ring. Slowly and in unison at first, then the longer they all rang – the quicker the pace of ringing. All were chanting and clapping in unison!
Finally the chief Priest performed another Arathi – and all completed in a grand display of total and absolute devotion to Lord Shiva!

Eventually we all filed into the Mandir, very orderly – quite unlike the previous Temples.
There I was looking at this huge Lingam, and feeling the energy of all in the room. What great devotion was displayed to the mighty Lord Shiva!

The Lingam was garlanded, the 'offering' accepted, and then some prasadam was given back to me!
Then I prayed and touched The Lingam with both hands a few times, and paid homage to 'her' in all 'her' glory!
Finally a Priest gave me some Holy Water, so yet once again it was poured over the Lingam.
It felt as though this was the ULTIMATE Experience!
Not only had I enjoyed the bliss of the Puja beforehand, but also enjoyed my own *intimate* experience as well!

Just prior to this, before the Arathi, when I had asked Baba for a *special* gift – everywhere I looked – I mean everyone and everything was Baba – the walls, floors, devotees, and flowers in the hair – ALL WAS BABA!
He laughed and said – 'What would you expect –
I AM ALL – I AM LORD SHIVA AS WELL!'

Om Namaha Shivaya.

Scenery – let us talk about the scenery.

Hills and valleys covered by dry red dust, with sparse vegetation to say the least. Mostly thatched and shingle roofed huts / houses, surrounded by goats and livestock.

Women, men and small children, either planting crops or ploughing fields. Obviously in most instances not a school in sight.

The roads were unbelievably bad – to be expected I guess, in such isolated areas.

Interesting – upon reflecting, similar in terrain to parts of Egypt, Peru and Tibet.

At one stage we encountered three small children, aged about 3, 4 and 5 years approximately, walking barefoot on the side of the road, shielding their faces with an old scarf. The two younger ones holding the ends, and the one in the middle lifting the scarf out like a veranda.

The temperature must have been around 42-45 degrees.

As soon as we left Madhya Pradesh, the greenery began and the roads became better. All flowing, now we are in Gujarat.

Listening to Baba's students chanting the Vedas on my new purchase – a walkman. All well and happy in my little world – way up here on the roof of the world again.

The sun is setting and the sky illuminated by the rays. Everywhere I look all green and lush.

Both drivers and the car struggled through great adversity today. The air-conditioning going non-stop as the temperature outside was scorching hot! Still all is as it should be I guess.

Interesting – my Baba and Christ Medallion I bought from Whitefield, fell from my watch, so the Hotel cleaners will find a surprise!

Also the picture of Baba – a very serious one, that was stuck to the back of the passenger's seat – right at eye level for me, fell off today. I assume I do not need or require 'things' to remind me of 'Who' I really am!

Feeling deeply peaceful and fine.

Well, well my dear, so all is well in your Physical, Emotional, Mental and Spiritual World?

I think not!

You have been remiss in your communication with me.

There is still too much 'I' connected to / with your work.

You do the preparatory work I ask you to do before you arrive at your Jyotir Lingam Temple.

Next you must FOCUS on only what I say – not what others are doing / saying / thinking.

You are AN INSTRUMENT OF THE LORD – not of / for others at this stage of your Spiritual Life, as you know it to be.

If I say 'Stop the car NOW – You stop!'

You do not listen to ANY others at this stage of YOUR growth.

Now enjoy the bliss of the setting sun – I am much pleased with you some of the time – at other times you can be a thorn in my side.

You feel upset with my statement?

Remember my dear – with every thorn a rose will bloom.

Soon you will flower into the most Divine Bloom.

Soon my dear – soon.

Do not waste time – time is not on your side at *this* stage of your Spiritual Journey.

You do not need my pictures – I AM YOU – YOU ARE ME – TOGETHER WE EQUAL ONE.

More focus still my dear – then let us see what eventuates.

Yes, you experienced childlike wonder when you saw my
Form on everything you looked at this morning in the
Temple. Just a little something to ensure your love in me
stays centred and strong, with no room for compromise –
understand?
Yes, I feel you do!
Rest my dear – I am much pleased with you – but more
FOCUS still I beg of you.

16.06.06.
8.08a.m.

Regarding the trip!
My body is so sore – my back and legs aching and throbbing,
from yesterday's work and travel.

Irene my dear – listen carefully now.
You are still not with me 100%. It is not YOU doing the
work – IT IS I – Baba doing the work.
So, release the 'I' – Your Ego – and all will flow, or let us
say – Your Journey will be smoother.
Now let us review the situation.

You must not drive for more than 8–10 hours – only 12
hours for emergencies.
Three star hotels in small towns will be fine for you.
Drink *more* water.
Do not drink coffee / tea from outside or from other's
drinking vessels.
Fruit – mangoes and papaya are everywhere – what
happened yesterday?
Bananas can be kept in the car daily.
Extra water – fruit juices and nuts.
On any rough stretch of road you must sit in the front of
the car for back support.

Buy an extra cushion.

Book ahead if you are running behind time.

Arriving at hotels at 11.00 p.m and then you ask for a good price! You have no bargaining power at that time of the evening.

Regarding The Temples:

You do the 'inner' work first, then find a quiet stretch of road and write about the experience.

Once in the line – no talking to your driver or another.

Just Focus – FOCUS – Listen to only MY VOICE.

The voice of illusion some say – the voice of God others say!

You must have your own 'money' ready to give freely of with love.

If you require for the car to stop whilst you write your 'inner' story – THEN STOP THE CAR!

Your driver is not in charge – you are!

Who then is in charge of you all?

Yes, I AM THAT I AM.

You will re-enter the Divine flow at 12 midday today.

Om Sai Ram.

You ask Baba if I am upset with you?

Yes, a little – you are nowhere near your FULL potential, and as I previously said – TIME IS NOT ON YOUR SIDE!

The MORE you focus on Me – MY TRUTH ALONE – the easier your travels will become, the higher your Energy, and the more abundant the flow of Love in your direction.

IT IS YOUR TRUTH ALONE THAT WILL SET YOU FREE!

MY TRUTH – YOUR TRUTH – GOD'S TRUTH!

FOCUS IS THE DIRECT ROUTE TO SALVATION.

Wait until midday – and then SEE AND FEEL how much you are loved.

17.06.06.
8.17 a.m.

Well here I am on the way again after a rather pleasant day, not many hours of travel thank goodness.
A relaxing stay in Rajkot at The Imperial Palace – the hotel one of the best I have stayed in thus far. The staff so friendly and trying to help in any way they possibly can.
Am I the only Westerner travelling in India? One would think so! With the exception of two married couples, I have not encountered any others on this trip – especially at the more affordable hotels.

After the gruelling work of the first few days Swami said 'Stay in the best Hotels, and leave the financial burden for me to bear!' So that is exactly what I am doing!

Yesterday evening I stayed at The Meridian Hotel in Ahmedabad, Gujarat. Apparently it was originally The Holiday Inn, and taken over a few years ago. I found it to be very expensive and not nearly as beautifully appointed as The Imperial, where the girls on reception were ever so friendly and helpful.
All in all an interesting experience though!

Awoke about 4.00 a.m. after another 'telling off' from Swami on LACK OF FOCUS! I felt as though Swami had left me momentarily, and was actually thinking – was the trip worth completing – where is this all going?
IS THIS ALL AN ILLUSION?
Can ONE Soul actually help alleviate Global Suffering, and by some miraculous conception of realization, help save *some* Souls from a fate worse than death?

I felt abandoned, weak, aching limbs, thighs, very painful lower back, with my lip still sore and bleeding, skin lined and very dry.
Why must God's work be *so* hard?
Then the voice of God / Swami / Sai boomed back 'Because you have NOT surrendered to me completely'!

So I made a pact to try to focus once more. Then began yet once again to experience amazing visualizations and thought forming patterns.
There I was as Irene, lying in bed asking Swami for help – then there appeared in the sky a huge Space Ship. It landed – the steps unfolded downwards, and then Swami was at the open door beckoning me 'Come quickly, you are late!'
After travelling some distance we landed.
This is Utah,' He said, and so it was.
Those amazing tablelands one sees in the photographs.

We were standing in front of a huge rock, when the rock slid open, to reveal the most magnificent blue Sapphire Crystal – many faceted, and gleaming, like you see in the Jewellery Store, not rough cut and natural. It was resting on a pedestal about waist height – the actual stone about two feet high and one foot in width – shaped more like an oval – egg shaped cylinder.

Then I was told to ring Valerie Barrow – the author of the book 'Alcheringa' – The Creation of the first Ancestors.
Briefly I experienced some moments of Egypt, even though Baba had said we were in Utah.
Then Baba said 'Keeper of The Crystal Grid.'
'The Stone People encased in the Pelvic Rim'.

There I was standing looking at this amazing crystal, illuminated like a diamond – wondering exactly the significance, and what I would do?

Baba then said 'You are The Key.'
I didn't quite understand.
'You are The Key to unlock The Crystal!'
I still didn't understand.
Then he said 'You are The Code!'
I still had no idea what to do or say.

Then I saw my body change and become like a computerised,
numbered Key. My whole body – the shape of a Key, but in
Human Form – more like a computerised 'Form' of Recognition.

**Remember how you are lying or standing NOW – as that
will be YOUR Key!
16 OTHERS have a Key also!'**

Apparently Valerie Barrow has a Master Key.

**So my dear, an interesting night when you FOCUS ON
ME!
All of your stories you have not transcribed – as you watch
rubbish on TV, then fall into negative compounded
unconsciousness and exhaustion!**

**So bathe, food, writing, and listening to my every word is
your evening duty!
Yes, you have one of the 16 Keys – TO OPEN THE DOOR
TO SALVATION FOR MANY, and to open up a 'can of
worms,' for many others.**

**The Sapphire Crystal / Stone encased in the Pelvic Rim of
ALL Mankind – is The Key you have all been looking for!
You search here, there, everywhere – and yet it is nowhere
you all search, because it is an INTERNAL Key!**

Deep within the Pelvic Rim of *most* mortals lies an 'unlocking' device or Key, to allow you all direct access to the God within, NOT WITHOUT!

No, it is not to do with the Heart or Soul of Man.
Indirectly of course – ALL is to do with the Heart and Soul of Man. This is to do with the 'nature' of Man and his Ego!
The Ego lies in the mind of Man you all think!

Wrong!
The Ego is the DNA Essence of Self locked in every cell; it just is controlled and converted to a 'thought process' by the Mind of Man.

The actual Key to unlock the Cellular Memory or DNA Patterning, is hidden within the cellular structure of 'The Pelvic Rim!'
The Crystal Grid Sapphire is a Coded Transcription of the very 'Essence' of Man – ALL MAN OR MANKIND.

It is The Key to unlock verily all aspects of the Negative influences of Mankind / Humankind /Animal kind.
It has a cellular restructuring capability with a molecular break-up facilitation process, or DNA Likened Suffragette Patterning.

'Likened Suffragette Patterning,' occurs when the DNA itself tries to overextend its own complexities and becomes limited in its Universal Intent. Hence it is incapable of altering the Molecular Structure it has maintained, and needs NOW to be released.

So as the Energies, Frequencies and Vibrations increase, the DNA should also accommodate these changes and accelerate accordingly.

Yes, it modifies to 'a degree' but incapable of *true* modification with *exact* Universal Intent.

You all have The Key – it is what you have all been searching for!

Irene asks – what about only 16 having The Key?

No, 16 have The Key to 'unlock' the Crystal Grid Formation of Man.

5 of the 16 have already been activating the 'Crystal Grid' for the last 3-7 years.

Hence the ability for *some* to convert easily their own DNA, to maximize their full Spiritual Empowerment and Acceleration.

So all of you reading this – just visualise the Sapphire Crystal in the Pelvic Rim and see what eventuates from this experience!

Om Sai Ram.

So tonight my dear you will complete your Crystal Grid Work, to help with the 'upliftment' of Humanity.

Now release all of this, as you have *other* work to do – Shiva Work – for Mankind.

NAGESHWAR
Taluk, Maharashtra

17.06.06.

LINGAM 8 – NAGESHWAR.
Taluk, Maharashtra.

Supriyuda was an ardent devotee of Lord Shiva.
Dakurudu, a demon, developed hatred to Supriyuda, so attacked and captured the merchant ship he and his fellow merchants were on. Supriyuda prayed in earnest to Lord Shiva to save the other merchants, with little regard for his own safety. Shiva was very pleased with such devotion and prayers, and gave him a Divine Weapon to kill all the demons. It was at that place Lord Shiva installed himself in the form of the Nageshwar Lingam, and Parvathi was known as Nageshwari.

Today we are on the way to the eighth Jyotir Lingam.
Remember the eighth for me on my travels, but not in the exact order 1-12 for the normal traveller and their experience.
Swami says to travel The Jyotir Lingams 1-12 in order is the best for our Spiritual Acceleration, however as this can be a

longer and more torturous route for me – this way is fine – it just means I will have extra energy work to do at a later stage.

Coffee break – an interesting place.
Swami has said no tea, coffee, samba, or chutney – only normal food for a few days.

THE INNER-VIEW:
What do I see through my *altered* vision?
A Circle equally divided into three equal portions or triangles, with a hole in the middle – or a very small 'inner' circle.
Now it is changing. The centre is directly linked to the Jyotir Lingam by a thin fragile energetic blue line. In two places the energy so faint it almost appears to be broken to the normal eye. However, it is just that the density is *so* fine.

Now from the middle of the circle – looking from underneath, the triangles are forming a pyramid. The apex of the pyramid now touching the Jyotir Lingam.
'AS IS ABOVE IS BELOW' Swami just said.
The Lingam has a Crystal Grid Frequency Network of 22 – whatever that is. Oh dear – all Jyotir Lingams have their own 'Frequency Network'.
Apparently this work will be done after all Jyotir Lingams have been visited – the 12 complete!

The energy below the Lingam once again blocked and convoluted.
Where the points of the Pyramid and Lingam meet the energy lines are off centre by 0.03% – not a huge amount, but difference enough to destabilize the energies at this particular Lingam area. The slight difference begins as 0.03% then at the base of the pyramid extends to 3.00% – a huge difference in energetic terms.

Amrit will flow from the Eyes of Parvathi after today's work.

Amrit: Immortality granting nectar – with the consistency of honey.

From the outside the Temple is magnificent both architecturally and in stature, and hosts examples of all the 12 Jyotir Lingams in its grounds. There are many Shrines to see, however apparently the 'sulking' Statue of Parvathi with Shiva, is the one to really look for, after viewing the Jyotir Lingam.

Yet once again I am confronted by Swami, talking about and showing me visions of the Sapphire Crystal Grid Formation!
The Crystal Grid inside the glorious Sapphire has 108 facets.
Then Swami and I were standing directly in front of the 'open' Sapphire. He then reduced me to the same size as the sapphire.
It was about 2 feet tall. So there I was inside, then it closed.
I became fearful, and asked Swami to open it. It felt uncomfortable being reduced in size, so Swami increased the size of the crystal to enable me to comfortably walk around inside.

I am now inside The Blue Sapphire Crystal, and looking at the 108 facets. They contain ALL Knowledge of ALL Universes!
Apparently when ONE of our Crystal Grids line up with The Universal Intent, then THAT Knowledge will be absorbed and reactivated by our DNA.
It is as though we absorb back into the Essence of Self, the Knowledge we already contain and know.

OR ANOTHER DOOR OPENS – AND SOON ALL DOORS ARE LEFT OPEN!

It is likened to THE GREAT AWAKENING!
Can we all attain this Higher Knowledge?
Apparently YES – once the 16 Keys have been activated to unlock the Crystal Grid Formation at *this* particular time, in the history of the Universe.

Is it just 'our' Universe you all ask?
No, all Universes work concurrently or simultaneously to line up with The Global Transmission Numbers, and their individual identities.

This is all quite complex for the average reader to understand you ask?
No, not really, as only those who are meant to attend to *this* work will be interested in reading *this* particular work. Many out there *know* this knowledge, but as yet many are reluctant to verbalize and write about it.

Yes, the 16th yesterday was very important for you – You were meant to meet The Dalai Llama.
Because of extenuating circumstances, your journey was delayed, so I attended to the work on you as ordained.

Yes, it was 'The Mantra' for awakening of The Crystal Grid Formation you missed. I will see that you have The Mantra soon!
Amma, the Divine Mother knows The Mantra, but will she give it to you?
We will see.

Does The Blue Sapphire Crystal have anything to do with THIS particular Lingam?
Yes, all 12 Jyotir Lingams contain 'specific' Knowledge you will ALL soon be given.
So, 12 Jyotir Lingams with 108 facets.
Or 108 divided by 12 = 9.
Yes I am laughing – IT IS MY NUMBER – The Swami Number – the LOVE vibration of number 9.

When the 12 Jyotir Lingams have ALL been activated for the benefit of Mankind, THEN the facets of The Crystal Grid Formation will be installed, and then ACCESSIBILE for ALL Mankind.

Patience, patience my dear one, all will unfold in due course.

So you cannot let the Monkey Mind rest my dear?
Do these Lingams contain the Blue Sapphire Crystal inside?
We will talk about that later – after you visit the Temple and The Jyotir Lingam.

Om Sai Ram.

I am much pleased with you today; you are back on track, and no coffee either!
Good girl – fruit juice and soya milk for you.

1.15 p.m.

My Australian mobile phone has always been switched off on this trip, and just a moment ago it rang. It was Valerie Barrow. Why am I not surprised!
So we discussed The Crystal Blue Sapphire and Grid Network. All very interesting – but a bit limited, as I was in the car with the drivers.
We discussed the 108 facets and the 12 Jyotir Lingams =1296, and talked about the significance of these numbers. Then we finished the conversation. Three minutes later Swami said, '1296 divided by 9 = 144!'
WELL THERE IT WAS!
The 144 from The Bible – Wow!
This is all amazing – well to me anyway I guess.

We are nearly at Nageshwaram, so will write more later.
Oh yes, I rang Valerie Barrow and she laughed – 'I was wondering where the 144 was?'

I am very happy Swami – happy, happy!
Thank you for a glorious morning.

The description from the Internet of The Nageshwaram Temple
and Lingam were vastly different. I came expecting as per one
of the descriptions, and realized my expectation had in fact
coloured my viewpoint.

First of all The Temple was away out on an isolated point – with
the sea on both sides.
Then as we rounded a point of reference, the most beautiful
Shiva Statue towered over the trees and shrubs alongside the
Temple. It was truly amazing in colour, and indeed quite awe-
inspiring!

Into The Temple area, where Baba had me spend liberally on an
offering – flowers, special water, two coconuts, many silver
coloured lotus petals, two silver coloured snakes – cobras, and
sweets.

I waited patiently for two families to complete their Puja.
Finally into the main inner sanctum, and right beside the actual
Lingam.

It was the most glorious of times! I prayed, touched, blessed and
gave thanks for the opportunity to be so close, and then placed
the silver coloured Lotus Petals on top of the Lingam, which the
Priest gave back as prasadam.
This was followed by the two silver Cobras – also taken back as
prasadam.
With my Shiva Ring I touched The Lingam – the top, base, sides,
and then garlanded it with flowers and coconut.
The Priests asked my surname – two of them chanting the whole
time.

On completion of the Puja, two of the lotus petals and one cobra ring were placed at the feet of Parvathi, right beside The Lingam. I asked The Divine Mother for forgiveness and for any wrongs I had done to her in any way – past, present or future.

As I walked out of the inner sanctum, I realized I had enjoyed the whole area to myself, and no-one had in fact been with me – with the exception of the Priests, for most of the time.

During the actual touching of The Lingam, the SHIVA Energy surged through my body and exploded forth into extensive periods of trembling and shuddering.
All in all – a very powerful experience.
Indeed I am blessed!

It's interesting just observing myself. I'm feeling so much stronger today – almost reborn. I can't seem to put my finger on what has happened exactly, but feel as though I must have absorbed 'something' from the visit into The Blue Sapphire Crystal.
Is this so Swami?

Yes, this is so – and only a small area of your actual DNA Regime has been altered.
Even just a few moments within the Crystal, and the Energy absorbed by your cells altered the molecular structure of the DNA.

THE INNER-VIEW:
What happened with the energy and shapes I saw?
After the Puja and chanting, Mother Earth changed her vibration ever so slightly, allowing the Energy from below the Earth to expand upwards into the faint Energy line I had previously seen. It became more dense and concentrated in appearance.

Then just after 1.15 a.m. this morning, I saw the Energy lines connecting a Pyramidal shape to the Lingam.

Suddenly there was a huge explosion, and the energy from The Mother surged through The Lingam into the top portion of the triangle / pyramid, and broke through the walls and out into the circle – surging through these walls out into The Cosmos.

However, on another level, at the very same moment, the same was happening below The Earth.
I could literally see The Earth move, as vast currents of underground pent-up energy began to flow.
For a brief moment I thought of CALAMITY – then realised ALL would ultimately be for the good of Mankind.

We spent the night at Porbandar in the fantastic Hotel Kaveri International. The staff were ever so friendly, a fair price, and the service was excellent.

Do you have any news Baba?

Yes my dear – First of all this should have been written about last evening – I will say no more!

**Regarding the Energy Shifts and Earth Changes –
I am using your Physical Body only as a CONDUIT for 'My' Energy at this time. After all, I AM SHIVA – I AM ALL!
So you think – Monkey Mind – Ego, you are touching and paying homage to The Jyotir Lingam – when in actual fact IT IS PAYING HOMAGE TO YOU – AS YOU ARE ME!
It is My Linga – ALL are My Lingas!
They are an aspect of Me – My Internal Dynamic Structure, manifested to create Harmony and Balance.**

Yes – as it was then – Demons and Negative Energies creating havoc in an otherwise peaceful time and place – SO IT IS NOW!

Millions have worshipped The Jyotir Lingas over thousands of years, however, due to Avataric Manifestation of Human, Animal and Environmental Rights – The Ego of Man began to REIGN Supreme.
Yes – back to the Ego yet once again!
It is all still related to Karma and Karmic Patterning.

I came, I saw, I gave, and did what I could to help save a worsening Global situation.
This is and has always been My Role – as Shirdi, as Sathya or Prema Sai.
This has also been My Role due to the manifold positions I pertain to programme the Universes in entirety.
So I have My Human Incarnations as Shirdi, Sathya and Prema; and My God Status as The ONE – SHIVA / SHAKTI – The Om – The Eternal sound of ALL – THE I AM THAT I AM!

So if I Sathya or I God, utilize Your Physical Body as a conduit for My Energy, there will be many 'aspects' of your 12 Jyotir Linga visits you will not understand as yet.

As you visit – I allow YOU to experience the Energy of TRANSITION – however in actual fact YOU ARE ATTAINING A GOD LIKE STATUS DOING THE GOD WORK I HAVE DELEGATED YOU TO DO.

So no matter how magnificent your visit may be, or glorious and wondrous and blissful Irene, you still see and feel your normal Energy surges and associated behaviour patterns.
However – You Irene – the Higher Self – The God Self – doing specific work on MY BEHALF have an entirely different experience.
This is my work – Shiva Work – Mother Earth – Goddess Work – and it is I – Your Baba doing the work through you

for the total and absolute betterment of Human, Animal and Environmental kind.

What you see through your third eye is only what I want you to see. In actual reality each experience at every Jyotir Lingam has an overall effect of raising the Consciousness of Man by 33.3%.

This will only occur when the Grid Lines of the 12 Lingams have been resurrected and patterned to a 'new' timeframe acceptable to today's manifested and associated problems: For Example – Bio-warfare, Bio-technology, Terrorism, and the proliferation of Life Threatening Disease – aids, anthrax and viral complications.

It is not as though the Energy is not potent. It has been and still is NOW, however there is no escape from Environmental Pollution, restrictions and death.

NOW drastic steps have to be taken to once again REDUCE THE EGO + RAISE THE EFV (Energy, Frequency & Vibration) OF MAN.

With heightened EFV → CA (Conscious Awareness) = PC (Planetary Change).

Your old equation yet once again.

Heightened EFV → CA = PC.

At this time in the Universe there are many aware of the state of the Physical World and Cosmic Evolution, as it is deemed to be. Many have come forth and WILL come forth to assist in and with the raising of the consciousness of Man.

Because of Your 'acceptable' EFV Ratio Range – unbelievably high to low – a rare commodity for most Humans at this time on the Planet – You are one of the ones helping with Earth changes at this time.

Your particular work right now is to reactivate TO MY CURRENT NEW TIME FRAME the 12 Jyotir Lingams in sequence.

Now I fully realise you are not visiting the 12 Jyotir Lingams in order. It just means more work at the end for you to do – energy and balancing work that is.
For most, it is better to visit 1-12 in order. It does not have to be on one trip, however this is optimum to maximize Spiritual Growth and Acceleration at this time. If you can only visit one, then begin with number '1' if at all possible. Otherwise huge energy, frequency and vibrational shifts may not always be of optimum benefit to / for you and others in your environs.

You ask about The Divine Mother?
Of course you are meaning Your Divine Mother – Amma, Srimad Sai Rajarajeshwari, the 10th incarnation of Shakti. Yes, the Parvathi influence will have a huge impact on Humanity and the Environment in general.

As Shiva – Yes it was Goddess Parvathi I longed to be with, however there are many aspects to the Nature and Divinity of Rajarajeshwari.
You may ask her to list all of her 'entitlements' so you have a still larger or expanded awareness as to 'Who' She Really Is!
It is SHE who will come to the fore – to help raise the Consciousness of Man in this new millennium.

You ask about her feelings to me as Baba?
Yes – She also has many Human qualities to conquer, even though She is truly Divine.
Divinity, Divinity – Yes still ALL degrees of Divinity. No more, no less.

Explain to her – She has been looking in the wrong place for recognition. Recognition begins now – not previously!

Only as I become more 'aged' and frail will others look for another God / Goddess. One who will fulfil their needs and yearnings.
I am having you ALL – SEPARATE from My Form –
FROM THE FORM TO THE FORMLESS.

Om Sai Ram.

SOMNATH
Veraval, Gujarat

18.06.06.

LINGAM 9 – SOMNATH.
Veraval, Gujarat.

Dakshaprajapathi had 27 daughters, and all were given to the Moon God 'Chandra' in marriage. Chandra only loved Rohini. The others became very jealous and cursed Chandra to suffer a disease. Chandra could no longer keep the coolness in the environment, and the Universe began to suffer from the heat.
Great celestial beings and sages all sought Shiva's counsel to help overcome Chandra's curse. Chandra prayed the Mrutyunjaya Mantra many times. Eventually Shiva came in the Lord Mrutyunjaya Form and blessed him.
However Shiva said that during the first fortnight of the Hindu calendar Chandra would gradually reduce his illumination day by day, and in the second half increase his illumination, until he became the full Moon.
Chandra praised Lord Shiva, and asked that he and Parvathi reside there for protection of the Universe.

Somnath – The Lingam of the Moon God or Soma.
Driving along, and looking at the energy and picture I see from
the sun at this particular Lingam.

THE INNER-VIEW:

The Sun has 9 Golden Cylindrical Rods / Rays of light / energy
extending forth. However the energy has been convoluted and
corrupted by eons of absorbing the darker energies or aspects
of Man.

The 9 Rods or Rays are quite powerful, crystallizing and
formalizing 'their' INTENT at the Lingam – then travel
downwards into Mother Earth. Even *these* rays of golden energy
are *still* quite powerful.

Up to date, this particular Jyotir Lingam has the most powerful
and seemingly – let us say – least corrupt energy. And yet I still
feel *no* pull towards it as yet. Actually today I feel at relative
PEACE – EQUANIMITY – no feeling either way.

THE ENERGY OF THE SUN CAN AND WILL TRANSFORM THE EARTH.

Looking at the lush green vegetation, as we near Somnath
Temple.
Feeling extremely sleepy – no energy at all, so I asked My Lord
for help.
'Come with me,' He said, and then we were standing in front of
The Blue Sapphire Crystal.
'Just go inside and absorb 15 seconds of Energy and information
from The 108 Facets.'
So I did – and now will wait to see what eventuates!

Apparently, this is one of the most famous of the Lingams, or
the most famous, and the first of the 12 Jyotir Lingams.
The Temple is situated in the most glorious position right beside
the seaside. Quite grand, ornamental, and exquisitely carved.

Apparently the Moslems destroyed most Temples over thousands of years. The work on this Temple was completed in 1951 after India gained independence in 1947, by the then Prime Minister. The splendour of the Temple only suffering in the materials used, from gold to silver, wood, and finally stone.

We all filed in – very orderly I must say.
No pushing, no shoving, and no wonder!
The actual Lingam was about one metre high and half a metre in diameter, however barricaded behind a restraining fence, about four metres away, from where I was standing.

There appeared to be no *associated* emotion with this particular Lingam. I felt cheated and robbed of the experience somehow! Even whist travelling towards the Temple, I did not feel as though this would be a 'highlight' so to speak.
Yet from this Jyotir Lingam – fame has spread far and wide.

Whilst walking away from the main entrance, a little while later, I was *drawn* to a small – minuscule shelter – side Temple – in the far corner. It was there I paid respects and homage to Ganesha and the Lingams.
Surprise, surprise! The energy was beautiful and quite powerful, and yet delicate as well.
Apparently the small stone carvings and carvings of Ganesha were taken from the original Temple.
All in all a beautiful experience.

What of the 'inner' level Baba?

Later my dear later.
The Energy is not good where you are sitting.
Please leave and sit in the car.
Sadness, great sadness my dear – I feel for you and all of
Humanity.

This Jyotir Linga was a natural phenomenon. An amazing energetic 'Spin-off' Pole. It was used as a reflector for The Star People, and was the original Gateway to the Stars. It was through *this* Lingam – Seers and Great Ones could ACCESS their Destiny.

And what was their Destiny?
Their destiny was to act as a 'launching pad' into Self Awareness – Nirvana – Enlightenment – God Realisation.
Did this eventuate?
Only briefly, as time and time again throughout history when 'The Divines of Old' were nearing their full potential, their progress was temporarily halted through civil or religious uprising and propaganda.
Eventually *that* particular Temple would be destroyed, and the cycle of rebuilding would begin once more.

You read today this is the 1st Temple.
NO – in actual fact it is the 9th Temple, and still maintains THE STATUS of Gateway to the Stars. However, not fully activated at this time.

Every time the Temple was rebuilt, the Grid, Energy and Soma Lines were temporarily distorted.
Time and time again – the energy shifted, graph display options altered, and the Gateway altered in *all* Dimensions.

In the year 1216, the Gateway was adjusted by ET Robotic Transference Energy, however this energy was only maintained for a limited period of time.

Since the late 1700's – The Gateway Energy has only operated on a scale – Human Time Frame Scale of 01.4186%.
This is an unbelievably small percentage you are asking?
Yes and No.

Yes, because Humanity required MORE opportunities for Spiritual Evaluation and Growth.
No, because we are talking about Linear Cosmic Time frame, NOT Human Time frame in actuality.
Human Time frame is an illusion – Linear Cosmic Time frame is TRUTH!

In percentage time it sounds small in your Time frame – but in Star Gate Time frame it is still an acceptable percentage.
On the lower end of the scale admittedly, but still acceptable by Cosmic standards.

Now relax and do your work for me please, then continue.

The land around this area is quite flat, with larger green areas under cultivation. Now I do not mean miles and miles, but larger by Indian standards so far. Also I have just observed there are no cattle or animals to be seen.

Ensconced in the hotel and back in the same town – Rajkot – once again at The Imperial Palace. Oh, to be back in luxury again. We are talking about luxury by small town / village standards here!
Bathed, clothes washed and pressed – even my shoes were cleaned!

This side of the hotel is different and yet equally as beautiful – roof tops and more rooftops.
The sky a threatening shade of grey – has the Monsoon Season begun already?

Immediately in front of my bed hanging on the wall, are two paintings of matching, heavily embossed and ornate Chalices.
The blue, silver and gold – Shiva Chalice on the left, and the red, silver and gold – Shakti Chalice on the right.

Both aspects of Baba in this incarnation, but they appear to be placed on the opposite sides!

Shirdi Sai – Shiva

Sathya Sai – Shiva / Shakti

Prema Sai – Shakti.

Both Chalices have amazing red ruby stones embedded in the stems.

Why are they in my room Baba?

Well my dear first of all you are looking at them from a mirrored perspective – so you were right to think the right Chalice should be blue – and the left Chalice red.

They are actually mirroring the both aspects of Self as ONE.

Yes, yes, it always takes two – to make up the Whole.

You know – positive / negative / hot / cold / peace / war.

Irene, listen carefully.

You have been remiss in your meditation with me, and yes once again from you I require – MORE FOCUS!

Your Chalice overflows with the love I have for you, and My Heart is Your Heart.

This has been an extremely difficult journey for a Woman to undertake thus far.

Extremely tiring – exhausting at times, and don't forget you are NOW working in many other levels AS ONE.

All together and yet individually as ONE as well.

Different work, different levels, all coming together AS ONE eventually.

Just a reminder with the two Chalices – that you are BOTH PARTS OF ME – not just Baba – the Male – 'supposedly' in Human Form.

I am all – Shiva / Shaki – The Sun / Moon / Earth / Stars.
Please 'open' yourself up to your further understanding
of 'Who' I Really Am!
Remember, even in this room – there are two matching
beds, two matching chairs, two matching bedside tables
and two matching lamps.
Please be aware of the 'pairing' of opposites.
I am your first Love.

Now back to this morning, and completion of the work.
From the Somnath Jyotir Lingam extend the 9 Rays or Rods of
golden light upward, and the exact mirror image downwards.
The Sun above connecting 9 rods of light to the Jyotir Lingam –
and 9 rods of light from the Lingam, connecting to Mother Earth
below.

What do these 9 specific Rays / Rods of Light represent?
Looking from the left to the right.

1. Alignment and Arraignment of all Universes in
   sequence.
2. The Rainbow Energy from your Universe and other
   Universes, extending in colour, consistency and
   diameter.
3. Chakra Alignment and Rebalancing for the optimum
   Spiritual Growth at this stage of Human / Animal / Plant
   Evolution.
4. Maintenance and Management of all Stars and
   Planetary Alignments independently, and then
   collectively coming together as ONE.
5. Balance, Harmony and Equilibrium of The Earth's
   Core and Atmospheric Pressures, to be released with
   vengeance.
6. Stars, Stars, and yet more Star Gate Agendas,
   Propaganda, Sequential Timeflow Experimentation,
   and The LUXOR Involvement and Management
   Strategies.

LUXOR: An independent 'means' testing of Timeflow Apparatus and Timing Chain Mechanisms capable of catapulting you into another Timeframe or Dimensional Shift, within The Realms of Possibilities.

7. Polarity of Opposites – Experimentation and Upliftment for your Planet and many other Planets you are yet to experience. This is linked into the Coding and Robotic movement.
8. Parallel Thought Transmission Services Management Teams. Many will come to experiment and KNOW how to be here, there, everywhere. This will increase dramatically NOW!
9. Yes, it is all only about ONE Code of Universal Conduct – LOVE – The Feminine aspect of ALL Creation.

The Mother will open her arms and embrace all who treat her with LOVE.
LOVE IS ALL THERE IS.
THERE IS NO STRONGER FEELING / EMOTION THAN LOVE.
THERE IS NO SUBSTITUTE FOR LOVE.
LOVE ENCOMPASSES AND EMBRACES THE 5 HUMAN VALUES – for all Mankind on the Earth, and on other Universes you will all soon come to know.

The 5 Human Values are the mainstay of all Humanity and all living things –
TRUTH
RIGHTEOUS CONDUCT
PEACE
LOVE
NON-VIOLENCE.

Truth be with you all.
Sathya.

Plenty of rest, however my lower back is really aching, and I feel as though an infection may be on its way – soon fixed by the Pharmacist. The cost of four high-powered antibiotics and four Lasix, only 30 rupees – less than one dollar! ALL medicines for any condition dispensed with ease, or so it appears to be. And the cost – well need I say more!

Awoke about 5.05 a.m. and asked Swami if he had worked on / with me? Well all pandemonium broke loose!
It was as though *all* in the Higher Realms had been just waiting to be asked!
A Space Ship appeared immediately, and I was strapped to an Emergency Stretcher.
'Make way – hurry – we do not have much time to save her – she is approaching BURNOUT!'
Up into the Space Ship they carried me – all were expressing great anxiety and some had tears in their eyes. They all looked like normal ETs, however their Energy was overwhelmingly gentle and loving.

'Quickly, quickly, she must be put into The Liquid Crystal Vat!'
So into The Liquid Crystal Vat I went.
It was amazing!
As my body entered – part by part, section by section, I became invisible. I could still feel my body, as I know it to be, however I could not see it!

I floated and floated until all of my physical body was covered by the glorious Crystal fluid, with the exception of my left ear.
'Quickly, help her, otherwise she will lose hearing in that ear.'
There was nothing anyone could do – they all looked very concerned, and then as if by magic my left ear covered as well.
Much jubilation occurred – everyone was extremely happy.
'Only 19 minutes she is allowed,' someone said.

I floated and floated – all happy and blissful.
At one stage I quickly re-entered my physical body to see if I
was all right. Yes, I was normal, then quickly transferred the
'Mind, Body and Soul,' back into the Liquid Crystal.

During this time I could see The Shiva Golden Trident through
my spinal column. It was bent at the lower back area. Finally it
was removed and straightened, and then re-inserted in a slightly
different way; however still within the spinal column.

It was during this time that I knew it would be THE BREATH
that would help illuminate the very Core of my Being.
The Breath – The Breath – Never underestimate the
ABSOLUTE IMPORTANCE OF THE BREATH!

Finally I arrived back into the body of Irene – safe in bed.
Before the experience the clock read 5.05 a.m. and afterwards
it read 6.36 a.m. It felt as though it had only been a few moments.
Still resting, I began thinking about the Sapphire Crystal in the
Pelvic Rim and also the Crystal in Utah – in America.

If the Crystal is embedded within the Pelvic Rim, then why did I
have to go to a 'cave' in Utah to see it?
Then I saw the base of it in the Pelvic Rim, and it was illuminating
white blinding light, with only minor traces of pale blue.

Suddenly it moved quickly upwards into the chest area to the
Heart, or just above, to the Seat of the Soul – and exploded into
the most glorious Rainbow Crystal I had ever seen.

I could not understand how it could be blue, white, and then
rainbow in colour. How could it change from the Cave → Pelvic
Rim → Heart → Seat of the Soul?
It felt as though it could expand right through my body to the
crown. Was it many different Crystals or was it ONE – that had
changed?

During the time in The Liquid Crystal Vat or Floatation Chamber, I was told I would be given 'extra' energy for the work ahead!

So – The Crystal Grid Network and changing colours?

Yes my dear, all an illusion of the Monkey Mind you think! Why are you all so limited in your appreciation in the Power of God Almighty? Limited, limited – I say!

ALL ARE LIQUID CRYSTAL – ALL are experiencing expanded awareness, and simultaneous lives and existences. Not just you my dear!

This book – new book – will OPEN UP A Pandora's Box of WITHHELD knowledge. Only after reading about your experiences, will some then be willing to look at 'Who' they Really are, or 'Who' am I Really?

With the sharing of knowledge and experiences comes – THE ULTIMATE FORM OF EXISTENCE – THE ALL – THE I AM THAT I AM.

Because of the extended and prolonged 'lapse' in Conscious Awareness – you all mostly live in a TIMEWARP OF THE PAST.

As the Energies, Frequencies and Vibrations elevate substantially, soon you will all experience this *new* way of being – an illumination of the 'true' God Force in all its splendour.
You will experience many thoughts, visions and experiences, to bring you ALL into alignment with GLOBAL HARMONY.

Global Harmony occurs when your own Energies, Frequencies and Vibrations elevate enough to line up with the Global Transmission Numbers.
THEN AND ONLY THEN – LOVE OR PEACE OR BOTH WILL REIGN SUPREME.

Regarding the Crystals now –
The 'Cave' in Utah was a transmission of thought. It was easier to get you to go 'inside' a cave, than experience going 'inside' yourself.
If I had said 'Go inside your own Crystal and Grid Formation,' you would not have understood.
Why in Utah you ask?
Because Utah is the actual Indigenous HOME of Crystal Grid Formation Complex Systems and ET activity – 'Paranormal Studies' – others say!

You all have within Your Own Essence – Your Own Truth. This 'Truth' expands to become THE ONE TRUTH – GOD!

Embedded deep within the Pelvic Rim is the base of your Crystal Sapphire. Shining blue to some, blinding white to others, and still yet different – RAINBOW to some others, at *this* time in your history.

Yes, it extends upwards to embrace the Heart and ALL Chakras – even above the head to the 13th Level or Enlightenment, at this stage of your Universal and Spiritual Growth.
So in actual fact you all ARE A CRYSTAL!
The reason you have seen 'some' with Crystals above their head – like a hat – is because YOU HAVE ALL BEEN SEEING ONLY THE TOP!

Deeper, deeper, you must all go – into *this* area of Knowledge that will ultimately set you all FREE!
Just relax, and we will speak later Irene, relax and be with your very own Crystal – Rainbow Child that you are!

Yes, yes, you are the 'smarty pants' as you would say – your new grandchildren are both of The Rainbow - The Crystal Rainbow Variety.

God Bless Humanity.

Just a reminder that all Crystals will 'appear' solid, but in actuality *this* is A GREAT ILLUSION.
When you look at / observe / see The Crystal Grid Formation of The Universe – remember it is a Movable Current – ENERGY!
ALL is movable – transient – and most definitely capable of CHANGE – intra or extra Cellular Change!

The importance of The Crystal Grid Network is the REFRACTION / REFLECTION OF THE LIGHT RAYS.

All you are observing now my dear is the 'Working of your Human Apparatus' on another level, that is all.
Nothing more – nothing less.

THE INNER-VIEW:
The Work at Somnath?
Very interesting and quite complex to explain.

As I mentioned previously the Sun – above the Lingam, and Mother Earth below. Imagine a ball of light above and one equi distant below. The 9 Rays / Rods come from the upper ball of light, the Sun, to the Lingam, then cross over at the point of

intersection – the Lingam. Then extend through the Lingam to
the opposite section of the lower ball of light – Mother Earth.

So as the Rays / Rods pass through the middle of The Lingam
they cross from the left side 1–9 to the right side 9–1.
For Example – Light Ray 1 from above, becomes Light Ray 9
below, Light Ray 2 becomes Light Ray 8, and so on.
It is as though they mirror the opposite of each other.

Yes my dear – indeed they do.
They correspond to their own Equivalent Value of Equals.
Quite a complex arrangement of equals I may venture to
say.

Due to huge Earth shattering Calamities – Underwater
Pressure Changes, this area has been subjected to huge
flooding and underground movement.
This area has been most unstable, emitting a varying range
of gases as well.
Poisonous gases you ask?
That is dependent on the amount of consumption.

Somnath was once the home of many who worshipped the
Jyotirlinga and bathed in the bliss of the Temple
surrounds.
With every destruction of the Temples and movement of
the Jyotirlinga – the pressure assimilation changes
increased dramatically.
As is above – IS BELOW!
A well of Love soon became a despondency of DESPAIR.
No amount of Worship / Homage / Chanting, could change
the dynamics of this particular Jyotirlinga.

The immediate solution to help Humanity and the
Environment at *this* stage, is to redirect the Energy of the
Sun to a corresponding pattern of equals, deep into the

Core of Mother Earth.
Then and only then, balance and stability WILL REIGN
SUPREME.

THE ENERGY OF THE SUN WILL TRANSFORM THE
ENERGY OF MOTHER EARTH AT SOMNATH.

Om Sai Ram.

20.06.06.

Glorious overnight stay at a hotel – similar in architecture to
'The Raffles' in Singapore.
To be able to open the windows and see and be with nature, was
truly wondrous.
Last evening I sat high up on the veranda and overlooked the
garden – rain falling, temperature warm, and enjoyed a glass of
Indian red wine with dinner.

Am I allowed to eat fish or chicken and still enjoy a glass of red
wine? Apparently yes, however this morning poor Baba is
suffering because of me!
My liver and body in general is still capable of digesting and
assimilating the alcohol or protein from the meat.
So, I enjoy and Baba suffers!
Well that is one way to prevent me from being so overindulgent
and selfish again!

Travelling north from Udaipur to Jaipur.
The scenery is quite magnificent. High, high hills with lush
vegetation – very steep and winding roads. Skywards we are
travelling, and then down into the valleys below.

Noting whilst driving – the main industry from Udaipur to Jaipur
is the marble and granite industry.

The land is more flat and dry, with vast amounts of marble dust hovering in the air. From a distance – almost looking like a 'haze'. Prior to this were crops of wheat, barley, groundnuts, kidney beans, and grasses for animal fodder.

Feeling quite loved today.
Claire is massaging my feet on the subtle level, with Varuni, Sue, Margot and Janice, all sending love and healing.
Just thinking about Janice and her relationship with Des – will they be together? A relationship based on friendship must surely be more viable and sustainable if and when romance creeps in.

Baba has been presenting me with car and motorcycle number plates as 'guides' to clear myself from Negative Energy.
Feeling fine and all well.

11.44 a.m.

More Somnath Work –
I saw in the subtle – Shiva's Trident piercing Mother Earth.

Releasing the Fire from the Belly of Mother Earth!
Yes my dear – this then is TRUTH.
Your Truth – My Truth – ALL IS TRUTH.

You enquire about – Releasing the Fire from the Belly of Mother Earth?
For decades, hundreds and thousands of years past, the energy of / from THE MOTHER has kept the Universe in a state of unmitigated passion, fury and splendour.
The reason for this is twofold –

1. Destabilization of the Axial Pole, therefore the destabilization of and to this Universe, and all Universes simultaneously.

87

When imbalance and disharmony reign supreme in ONE Universe, then 'this' destabilization is felt physically, and energetically on a Cosmic level. Remember – ALL IS ONE.

2. **Disregard and abuse of The Mother Earth, and ALL she represents.**
   Through massive pollution, denuding the forests, contaminating the water ways, fumes and gases, poisonous in the extreme, generated by toxic waste being dispelled by Man, and his 'supposed' necessary comforts in general.
   Those of you in positions of power and wealth have a lot to answer to / for.

Om Sai Ram.

21.06.06.
2.55 a.m.

Awoke before 3.00 a.m. and then about 3.03a.m. began attending to *more* Somnath Jyotir Lingam work.
The Energy, Grid and Lay lines were all cleared, tightened, realignment checked yet once again, and connected to the Axial Pole – from the centre of the Earth and into the centre of the Sun.

At the connection point to the Lingam, the 9 Golden Rays / Rods of Light, from both above and below, were looped up at either end of the Axial Pole, like crochet loops. Then the loops were tightened to become ONE, and inserted at the intersection – above to the Sun, and below to Mother Earth.

Eventually both ends were tightened until the 9 Golden Rays / Rods of light became ONE expanded Ray of brilliant light.

It was like an umbrella closing. The one expanded ray of light began to spin or rotate – slower and then faster. Soon the Axial Pole began to wobble, and became quite unstable.

Baba came in – 'Please SLOW it down quickly – it will take Human time of twenty-one days to adjust'.

Then I was shown that within twenty-one days it would begin to rotate at a slower and more even rate. Then balance and harmony would be reinstated.

I remember thinking – 'Where will I be in twenty-one days?'
Then smiled – at the highest point on MT. KAILASH!
Isn't God a marvel?
I think so!
I guess this is the reason I had to buy a back support yesterday as well.

Change of plans. We are leaving Jaipur, and heading towards Bihar to see another Jyotir Lingam.

Thought about going to Kedarnath first, but the timing is totally inappropriate, besides, the thought of a 14-kilometre walk is not for me as yet. In a few days I'll be feeling stronger hopefully.

The scenery yesterday was very mountainous – sheer rock faces and cliffs; extremely winding roads and sparse vegetation, not unlike central India.

Jaipur – The Pink City – Very historic, with many old and ancient buildings built from the pink stone.

Unfortunately no time for being a tourist – the time is only for the Shiva Lingam work.

This morning we will even by-pass Agra – so no seeing The Taj Mahal either.

No my dear definitely not on this trip!
Another place, another time – but definitely NOT now!

No distractions for you – as your FOCUS is still wavering, and not at its peak.
You awoke at 2.55 a.m. and did not write.
Your / My viewpoint changes over time, so if you are awake, please write then – not later!

Om Sai Ram.

Just drifting and resting, and then saw The Somnath Jyotir Lingam again. The energy exploded from the 'centre' Core and blossomed into the most extraordinary brilliance. Looking at this brilliance, and then watching it as it turned into the most glorious pink Lotus – 'The Hidden Wealth and Abundance of THE TRUTH OF AND FOR HUMANITY'.

12.00 midday.

Driving through the outskirts of Agra, my lumbar support from Jaipur a bit small and sliding up. Needless to say the road from Jaipur to Agra definitely was *not* smooth!

Prayed to God for a proper Lumbar support, and then around the corner next to the hospital, on the first floor, a Chemist with 'supports' in the window.
'Stop, stop,' I called to the driver, and then ascended the stairs. Eventually a perfect fit was found! Sitting up in the back of the car like a chirpy little bird now.
The car and drivers well – so all fine.

Thinking about the last three Temples and Jyotir Lingams. Apparently the State of Bihar has been divided since the year 2000 – so the Lingam is actually in Jharkhand now. Fortunately we are on a dual carriageway from Agra to Kanpur.

23.06.06.

Well – another day – another dollar – as we would say in Australia.
Yesterday – what an amazing day.
Why am I not surprised?

Sitting up in bed watching the Sun rise in all her glory from the
5th floor – the top floor of the Taj Ganges Hotel.
So Sunita – Angelina bobs around the world spreading light and
love, and helping others to find accommodation and protection
at the 'right' price.
What is to become of my friend?
Will 'the love of her life' finally arrive soon?
I think so!

Many will come to knock at this particular door.
A woman of enormous great beauty, and inner wealth; soon
to be matched by her outer wealth.

A Princess, Goddess and Queen in many past lives – this
you can recognize immediately. However the 'pure' love
she NOW has in her heart was refused, because of her
past lives in dire need and poverty.
So the 'poverty' that once was – is no longer – and NEVER
WILL BE!

In this lifetime she was born into grandeur and will depart
from this world attaining a far greater height in all areas –
physical, emotional, mental and spiritual.

She has within her grasp the ability to redirect Finance
and Foreign Trade for India at Government levels. She
should attain no less than this, in this her LAST lifetime
on Earth.

Om Sai Ram.

5.15 a.m.

The Sun – orange and gold in colour, has just risen.

Glorious – just plain glorious! There is no greater beauty than the rising sun.

The birds are flying past my window, as I look over forty acres of parkland. What great, great beauty the rising sun beholds. The orange of the sun now turning a blinding yellow.

My room is fit for a Queen. Burgundy and gold – elegant and yet purposeful in its intent.

VISHWANATH
Varanasi, Uttar Pradesh

23.06.06.

LINGAM 10 – VISHWANATH
Varanasi, Uttar Pradesh

Mahavishnu prayed to Lord Shiva to protect the Universe from evil and natural calamities. Lord Shiva granted his wish. After marriage, Parvathi asked Lord Shiva to take her home to HIS place in the Himalayas, but he moved to Varanasi.

Varanasi figures prominently in the epic – The Mahabharat, and is reputed to be at least 3000 years old.
Varanasi is the city that enshrines the very Essence of Hinduism.
The original name of Varanasi or Benaras was Kashi – derived from Kasha – meaning bright.
Varanasi's principal attraction is the long string of 'Bathing Ghats' lining the River Ganges – a pilgrimage place for those seeking atonement in the form of a 'cleansing' dip in the river.

93

Yesterday – we arrived at the outer area of Varanasi / Benares, later in the afternoon, then right in front of my very eyes – a huge sign to Vishwanath Temple.

The driver had already decided that we hire a guide, however as it was only 3.5 kilometres away, we headed straight there.
It was not easy to find by Western or Indian standards!
Parked the car, and then caught a cycle rickshaw, and soon we were at the 'lane' entrance.

Encountered many tours and tourists – mainly Indian.
The lovely man who sold flower garlands looked after my shoes.
It was at this point a younger man – a guide, befriended me.

'No Women – Foreign Women, are allowed inside the Temple, besides – you need to be a Hindu,' was the cry from all!
Tourists visit the 'other' Temple. Oh dear, I momentarily thought, and then remembered Baba was with me!
So up to the Police Guards I went.
My driver explained in Hindi that I was writing a book on the 12 Jyotir Lingams. After much deliberation, passport and visa checking, I was allowed entry to the Temple. It was here a police woman checked for mobiles. More thorough than airport security – even my ballpoint pen was checked!

Finally into the actual Mandir and up to the Jyotir Lingam.
A stern looking Priest was presiding over the Lingam.
He motioned for me to sit down next to it, and then to pour the milk I had brought with me, over the top.

After praying, I garlanded the Lingam with flowers and leaves.
Oh what great beauty and wealth of love was there.
Not millions of tourists or problems – just order and peace.
After receiving prasadam from the Priest, I humbly moved away.

Encountered a few minor problems trying to find the car, and with street vendors.
More money for the 'Puja' items – you know – the usual kind of thing. Finally back to the car, and guided back to the hotel by an auto rickshaw driver, for just a few rupees.

After a brief discussion with my drivers it was suggested to utilise the auto rickshaw driver to go to The Ganges at 7.15 p.m. for the Sunset Puja.
So off to The Ganges – towel in hand, just in case.
After seemingly many kilometres of winding lanes and small roads – some only accessible by very small auto rickshaws, we arrived at a main Ghat, on the banks of The Ganges.

Down the steps to the water's edge, where the driver and myself sat alongside the Priest, who was in the process of performing a Puja to The Mother – THE DIVINE MOTHER – The Ganges!
Finally we washed our hands, feet and head, in the water of Purity and Love.

All who 'die' here attain everlasting life or MOKSHA.
All who are 'born' here – attain MOKSHA – never having to return to play out another Human life of suffering.
All who 'live' here – good / bad / priest / criminal – all attain everlasting Glory – IT IS WRITTEN!

Yes, this is so.
In Past Lives ALL have incurred some form of 'troubled'
or Negative imbalance within the very cells of their Being.
ALL – I say.
If you were ALL perfect – YOU WOULD NOT BE HERE
ON THE EARTH AT THIS TIME!
Praise Be in The Name of The Lord.
Amen.

You come to The Home of God, you seek great love and respect for another, and yet you do _not_ respect YOURSELVES!

So, Who Are You Really?
You are verily God!
Is this not so?
I THINK IT IS!

Please be aware of Your Goddess Self – not just your Humanness!
It is your God Self that will sanctify your Soul – and show you the way Home – Not your Human Self!

Om Sai Ram.

9.29 a.m.

Plans have changed! We are not driving to Patna – the capital of Bihar, we are to go to Dhanbad in Jharkhand instead – a safer route, and definitely NO driving after sunset! We are to stay on the main highway – Highway 2 to Calcutta.

Regarding The Lingam – there are still no visions coming.
Why?
Apparently I am still stabilising the Axial Pole from Somnath.

Stopped at Reliance A 1, for a quick breakfast, however soon many vehicles of local people arrived, for a celebratory breakfast with the police. A local political party win I believe.

We have been advised to bypass Amahgabad, so will try to arrive somewhere safe before nightfall!
Swami says 'See the God in ALL, and ALL will be well'!

Varanasi is a 'Beacon of Light' – calling ALL Lost Souls home!
Souls who have passed over, and Souls that are still Earth Bound.
It is the foremost NATURAL Wonder of The World.
Hardly recognizable to the Mortal – Human Being, as ONE of the foremost Wonders of The World, however on a Spiritual Level – The ABSOLUTE PINNACLE OF ALL THERE IS!
The Om – The Sathya – THE I AM THAT I AM.

Aum Saayee Swaraa ya Vidma yee
Satya Devaya Dhimahi
Thannah Sarvam Prachodayat.

It is also the foremost and brightest STAR OF ILLUMINATION in the Galaxy.
It is a five-pointed Star – elongated in shape and contour, acting as THE DIRECTIONAL BEACON for The Universe.
The light emanating from Varanasi / Benares is singularly the brightest light there is or ever will be, on Earth in this Universe, and other Universes as well.

From the Core of the Star radiates the optimum vibration of Truth, Righteous Conduct, Peace, Love and Non-violence, Grace and Service to and for Humanity.

It has a Frequency – Vibrational Frequency of 33-40 repeating, at this stage.
Yes my dear, an Energy, Frequency and Vibration change is in order, so this is what you must do.

Change The Coding to accommodate the new 'change' ranges from your work at Somnath.

Oh I see you smiling – all coming nicely together now you are thinking.
Please do NOT use your Monkey Mind at this late stage.

The Circles of Energy you see will alter also the Tides and Weather Pattern for a period of 7-9 years, then ALL will stabilize and harmonize and come together as ONE. Each Beam or Radiation given out at this time is not as powerful or let us say fulfilling, on a Spiritual Scale, as the Essence of One.

The beams of light vibrating and radiating out from the Core, should radiate forth in a pattern of consistency – a certain amount of light being given off over a certain timeframe. In other words – in a quite orderly fashion let us say.

Until the work at Somnath was completed, this was an impossibility, as all Energy lines were incongruent. This was basically due to the partially decongested and convoluted Graph and Lay Lines, you have previously written about.

So your adjustments from Somnath will alter the Light energy, frequency and vibration aptitude and range from Varanasi. All good work my dear – all good work.
Look at this work later, when you are resting, and complete your writing then.

Yes, you are right – Bihar has massive Negative interference on many levels. Also do not become too complacent in Jharkhand because the grass is green, and the whole area 'appears' to be peaceful.
Remember, it was originally Bihar until the year 2000.
See what eventuates from your next Jyotir Lingam!

The Vishwanath Jyotir Lingam was reputed to be the FIRST ONE manifested by Lord Shiva's grace.

When Parvathi asked Shiva to take her to live at HIS abode, he took her to Varanasi. It was here they resided for a time as husband and wife.

Yes, yes, greater Love has no Man – than he lay down his Sword for the Love of God and the Love of a Goddess.

The feelings Shiva had for Parvathi – in all Forms, are still no different to those I experience in Human incarnation as The Purna Avatar of this Age.

God / Goddess – WE ARE ONE.

SOON IT IS SHE WHO WILL MANIFEST IN ALL HER GLORY!

Om Sai Ram.

VAIDYANATH
Deoghar, Northern Jharkhand (Bihar)

24.06.06.

LINGAM 11 – VAIDYANATH.
Deoghar, Northern Jharkhand (Bihar).

Ravana, the ruler of Lanka, chopped off his nine heads after Shiva refused to give him darshan. When he was about to chop off his tenth head Shiva appeared and granted him boons and restored his other nine heads.
Ravana was given the Atma Lingam by Shiva, providing it was not to be put on the ground until he reached Lanka.
On his way to Lanka, Divine Prayer time approached, so Ravana gave the Lingam to a small boy to hold. It was too heavy so it rested on the ground.
When Ravana returned he could not move the lingam with his physical strength, and left a thumb imprint on the top of the lingam. The impression is still there after thousands of years.

Well here we are on the way back to the Tourist Centre to stay the night, before our long trek back to Varanasi tomorrow.

The trip to see The Jyotir Lingam took five hours to cover 180 kms.

The terrain was some of the most beautiful I have ever seen. Green hills, gently sloping, and thousands of mud banks of 'Paddy' fields. Some not used for growing of rice, but for cattle feed. Cattle, goats, crops, all grazing and growing together in nature's world. Lush green vegetation, lakes, and abundant water – draining into the fields from somewhere.

However – the safety factor! Well let us discuss that, or the lack of safety, for the adventuresome traveller! Do not venture into uncharted waters if at all possible – especially in this area.

When Bihar was bi-furcated in the year 2000, I guess some would think the more politically unsafe areas were more towards the north – in the cities. Well today, during the visit to The Temple to see the Jyotir Lingam, the Energy was some of the darkest I have ever experienced so far.

Offers to do Puja from many, pushing, shoving, many asking for money, and that was BEFORE we entered The Temple. That was an exercise in itself! Then the real stampede began in earnest. All desperately trying to see and touch The Jyotir Lingam! Fortunately for me, I had left everything of importance in relation to value in the car. You actually require two drivers. One to be with you, and one to stay with the car for a speedy getaway! Safety – it is all about safety! 'The safety of One's Soul,' Baba just said.

The Lingam was garlanded with flowers, and the sacred water poured over the top. It was then I bent down and touched *her* in all *her* glory!

Yes, this Lingam is female in its intent, or rather it used to be.

PAST IS PAST!

The Energy of The Mother – no longer exists here!

The Shiva Energy was originally here to realign the Energy from two other Lingams – ones on a similar parallel or latitude.

In other words, when ALL THREE were in 'true' alignment, then the Energy of / from Mother Earth could flow in abundance.

All think – Monkey Mind / Ego – that all Shiva or Jyotir Lingams were only activated in relation to a Godly enquiry or requirement.

Yes, this is so in Heavenly terms or Divine terms, however as you would all 'now' realise – THE ENERGY OF THE DIVINE MOTHER IS ALL SUPREME.

IT GOVERNS AND COVETS ALL!

All look at the Godly aspect of The Lingams, however if you ALL *really* looked – you would see that there are many aspects to DIVINITY in itself.

Not just the stories relating to Gods, Goddesses, Divines, Negative Influences, Kings and Queens.

The main and most important underlying reason for The Jyotir Lingams being placed in such STRATEGIC POSITIONS throughout India, is no different to the positions of Stonehenge in the United Kingdom, The Great Pyramids in Egypt, or Macchu Picchu in Peru.

ALL are in the 'exact' correct Position – for the Highest Good!

THEY ALL FORM, OR ARE PARTS OF – THE UNIVERSAL GRID PATTERN TO HELP WITH THE

UPLIFTMENT OF HUMANITY FOR THE BENEFIT OF
MANKIND AT THIS TIME ON YOUR UNIVERSE –
AND OTHER UNIVERSES – YOU ARE ALL SOON TO
DISCOVER.

When are you all going to realise there are other Universes
'out there' far more intelligent and advanced, than you
appear to be at this time on your Earth.
You all think – Ego / Monkey Mind – I have attained this
or that 'Degree,' and some even pride themselves over
their achievements.
The only achievement I am at all interested in – is you all
accomplishing – stillness of thought, and incorporating The
5 HUMAN VALUES – Truth, Righteous Conduct, Peace,
Love and Non-Violence, into your daily lives.
Then and only then, these Basic Human Values can be
utilised in the Seva / Service, you need to aspire to give.

Help your fellow Man – help from a place deep within,
and from your heart with love.
Live in and with gratitude, if you have been blessed to
have attained a glorious standard of living and higher
education.
However – if you ALL choose to lead a Selfish Life rather
than a Life of Selfless Service – I WILL NOT BLESS YOU
IN THIS LIFETIME!

Even if you GIVE with the *thought* of Baba's Blessing as
an EXPECTATION, I will *allow* you to GIVE and you may
think I bless You – however this will NOT be Truth!
The only truth I am interested in is SELFLESS SERVICE
GIVEN FROM AN UNSULLIED HEART.
Do you hear?
I think so!

Now onto the Vaidyanath Jyotirlinga.
It contains the 'pure' energy from the State of Bihar only,
no other name or State.

The area around the Jyotirlinga – 100 square kilometres
is as dark or black as 'pitch.'
And you wonder why the people who live within this area
are so aggressive, and have *some* negative thought
patterning.

This Jyotirlinga carries the 'darkest' Energy of ALL The
Jyotirlinas in India.
It is void of GRACE.
It is void of TRUTH.
It is void of THE POWER OF ONE.

It has just become what it once was, and has been on
numerous occasions, during millennia of years.
It was primarily used as a Stabilizing Lingam – to balance
the other 11 Jyotirlingas.

The Negative Energy so potent and overpowering – it
could quite successfully at any given time, balance the
Negative Pole or Axis of The Universe single-handed OR
ON ITS OWN!

It is referred to in Spiritual Terms or Godly Terms as
THE GREAT NEGATIVE IMBALANCE!
Some refer to it as The Jyotirlinga associated mainly with
The Negative Karma of Man or THE NEGATIVE
KARMIC MANIFESTATION OF MAN.

Yes, I notice you touch your Heart, a headache of course.
That is not all you have in and around you, your drivers
and car!

So Recognize, Re-evaluate and Release – the 3 R's once again.
Then take rest!
Your *other* work you will attend to later.

This Jyotirlinga stabilises the effects of CORRUPT Negative Energy through the Axial Pole.

When the Energy of *this* Lingam is linked energetically to and with the energy of the other two, on the same latitude or parallel, the three come together as ONE – for the betterment of Man and with clear UNIVERSAL INTENT!

The stabilising effect of the three as ONE – pull into alignment the negative effects of the Axial Pole –
ALL = ONE.

Yes, it was to subdue 'The Ego' of The Demon King Ravana, that Rama descended on Earth. Not much different to now you are all thinking – and how right you are!

The Ego of Man will be the downfall and ruination of Man, and the crumbling vestiges of what will be left of The Earth, unless Man realizes the misfortunes and misguidance of his ways.

Man has no greater love at this moment in time, than LOVE OF THE EGO.
This is not to say *all* have Ego, this is just to say that *most* still have *varying* degrees of Ego.
You cannot undertake the Work of The Lord, with vast amounts of Ego.

Some confuse Ego with Self Confidence.

There is a subtle difference my Scholars and Worldly Ones!
Self Confidence includes Seva and Love for Humanity;
accomplished and attained from a pure heart.
It is confidence in ones own ability to perform Righteous
Endeavours, however only after One has SURRENDERED
to The Almighty Will of God – Divine Will!
Not Your Will – God's Will!

The Ego however recognizes the limitations and abusive
nature of Man, and manifests one hundred fold to try to
attain a 'worthy' status. When one is riddled with
insecurities, and low self-esteem, then one can try to
camouflage these 'hidden or overt' personality traits, by
utilizing THE POWER OF THE EGO!

The Ego has, and always will be The King / The Queen
over Man, unless he surrenders to God with NO
EXPECTATION, of or from a limited perspective of Man's
Truth.
It is not Man's Truth or Ego – It is God's Truth – LOVE!

Regarding The Jyotirlinga.
The Energy from The Lingam extends as a parallel in a
block of 100 square kilometres, also as a rod of light /
dark, from the East to the West.
It is this Energy alone, that has been, and currently is –
the most corrupt.

Om Sai Ram.

25.06.06.

Up early, and on the way back to Varanasi / Banares.
As we rounded a bend in the road I felt awestruck.
Before me stretched miles and miles of lakes, surrounded by

lush vegetation – trees and mountains. Immediately I thought of my friend Donna and Vancouver Island. If I had not known I was in India, it would surely have been Canada.

Thinking of Vancouver – The TRUE Heart of Man!

Five minutes later, and now once again on the main road. The junction of Patna and Calcutta Highways, turning left to Varanasi, and comfort for *one* night!

Yes my dear – The Spiritual Heart of Man – the very Essence of their Being – coming together as ONE.

All who 'divide' their loyalties in this lifetime – will struggle, as Opportunity soon, will only knock ONCE!

On completion of visiting The 12 Jyotirlingas, and you my dear doing exactly what I ask from / of you – you and many others WILL BE SET FREE!

However, will you attain final Release?

No, not as yet!

However the final 'tying-up' of the Energy, with the Energy of The Divine Abode – Mt. Kailash – will change the Energy of YOUR UNIVERSE and many other Universes simultaneously.

Can one single Human Being make such a difference you ask?

Yes, ONE can, dependent IF THEY CARRY THE ENERGY OF ONE – The God Energy.

However at *this* time, many are doing this work.

Not necessarily the way in which you have been asked to work – however work none the less – on a subtle – Cosmic Level.

You are thinking about a couple of your friends at home

praying for you. Yes you laugh – not many!
True, true, however do not judge them falsely as THEY
KNOW NOT WHAT THEY DO.

Many of your 'true' friends in India are praying for you.
Some even send you their *extra* Energy, when in fact they
do not have much to spare.

Yes, I hear you – You say, however you said this trip would
be joyous.
It is joyous!
However you do not see the great beauty and humour in
many, as you are still plagued by death, destruction and
toil.
If you were to relinquish or surrender those old thought
patterns and ALL negative Energy from your visits to The
Lingams, then you would experience *more* joy.

Joy is an illusion anyway.
What I require from you, is for you to remain in a state of
Equanimity.
Equanimity my dear – that is exactly what I require from
you.
Not overly outrageous – but a subtle exuding of the peace
of your commitment, to me Your Lord.
'Excellence in search of personification of The Truth.'

Please look now at yesterday's Jyotirlinga work and
expand on that.

Interesting – here I am just drifting, then after a discussion with
my driver, it *appears* we may not have enough time to visit the
last Jyotir Lingam. Not to mention driving to the airport on time,
to fly to Kathmandu for The Holy Mt. Kailash Trip! What – not
visit the last Jyotir Lingam? The work would be incomplete!

I feel fine – it will be a bit difficult, however to work under a bit of pressure is relatively normal for me most of the time. So I'll relax, and see what the good Lord presents.

Fear, fear, anguish, anguish – all is fine!
Time waits for no Man some will say, and yet TIME IS AN ILLUSION.
If I want to stop time – Time *will* STOP for me!
And you mortals are concerned about enough time to complete this journey, when you are attending to God's work!
I think not!

You all have time on your side at THIS time.
I grant you 'The Boon' of extra time, for this particular stage of your journey.
Sleep well tonight and be refreshed, as tomorrow I will make up your *lost* time!
Yes, the journey has been long and arduous. It was extremely important you partake of a Physical Journey at this point of your Spiritual Life. A life without adversity does not have the necessary effect.
This you would all agree!
Yes?

Give support and help to your driver and his co-driver.
They do not understand still as yet – The Magnificence of 'Who' I Really Am!
Baba – Your Life Saviour!

8.27 a.m.

Lying resting in the back of the car, or trying to – and asking for the vision of The Vaidyanath Jyotir Lingam.

THE INNER-VIEW:
Then I saw the 100 square kilometre area, and there Shiva appeared.
He 'paced' the 100 kilometres as though it were a few steps, and placed the base of his Trident firmly into the ground at each corner.
At each corner after 'tapping' the Earth, he blew his Conch three times.

Conch: A spiral shaped Shell.

As he did, the Earth below the Jyotir Lingam began to crack, and the four Energy lines from the middle of the Lingam went out to the area of the four corners, and began to clear the old accumulated waste energy.
The energy moved and poured forth from the outer area of the corners, into the central core of the Lingam – and down into Mother Earth.

Suddenly Shiva was standing at The Jyotir Lingam, and thumped the top of the delicate, shell-like Lingam with such force I thought the top would break.
He was clearing a pathway through to Mother Earth, for the 'old' congested and convoluted Energy – PAST IS PAST!

Finally vast amounts of 'old' Energy poured into Mother Earth.
However, it was as though the four outer points collected the 'waste' Energy, and then channelled it directly towards the centre of The Lingam. It was then dispersed into the Earth as ONE.
'So collected at the four corners of the 100 kilometre area, then directed into the main pipe or sewer,' Baba just said.
Sewer Baba?

Yes, Sewer my dear.
Rather than have the Negative Energies and Influences dispersed over many Jyotirlingas, it is better to amass

and then disperse Negative Karmic Influences – at ONE
Focal Point!
So it is NOW being prepared, and so NOW it will be done!

Mother Earth opening up and clearing the accumulated
waste – all kinds – from Humanity.
The mess you have all made and had to live with!
Now is THE TIME for Man to account for his indiscretions,
and be totally accountable for ALL his actions.
Then and only then will this Sewer of Misgivings – OPEN
UP INTO A WELL OF LOVE.

After a short period of time – more limited than any of you
would believe – your Sins will be absorbed then absolved.
The 'outpouring' of Human grief, sorrow and remorse,
will continue for a short span of time by My Standards.
Then all will dissolve INTO A WELL OF LOVE.
Then truth, righteous conduct, peace, love and non-
violence WILL REIGN SUPREME!

Om Namaha Shivaya
Om Namaha Om
Om Shanti Om.

The five Human or Life Values are and always will be –
THE MAINSTAY OF ALL THERE IS.
And what is there really?
The one Question you are all seeking the Answer to –
Who am I really?
Where am I going?
What will I be doing once I reach there?

The Eternal Question you are all seeking the answer to,
or is it THE ETERNAL QUEST?

Yes, it certainly is and has always been – Man's answer to
the Quest of – 'Who' I Really Am, or as you my dear would
say 'Who' Am I Really?
Rest now – more work for you to attend to later.

No, do not eat the *special* sweets, until you are on the
second part of your journey to Mt. Kailash.
Yes, the rose scent under your pillow or near your head is
a good idea for the evening.

The money I sent you – yes, you know what gift that is for.
You many choose Ganesha or Shiva, or the combination of
the both. You understand my meaning? It is only for you
to see and know what other beautiful apparitions I can
and will manifest for you, as a daily guide and means of
support.
Now rest.

You enquire my friend of the 'importance' of Somnath. Then
also the lightness and heart centre of Varanasi – and you
still ask 'Why not Puttaparthi – Prasanthi Nilayam – The
Abode of Eternal Peace'?

When an Avatar descends and embodies Physical Form –
like Rama, Krishna, even Shirdi – all go to a place of
prominence that is of prominence, at *that* time and space
in History.
'Each reaps its own Rewards,' so to speak.
On a Universal / Cosmic Level – Varanasi is and will always
be – The Lotus Flowering of The Heart – the *true*
illumination of the Light Force and Light of God.

Somnath will always be the meeting or convergence point
of all areas of Universal Understanding, in all Universes
simultaneously.

Prashanthi Nilayam – Puttaparthi, or wherever I reside at
that particular moment in time, is where –
THE I AM THAT I AM TRULY RESIDES.
So if I am in Brindavan – Whitefield or Kodaikanal, Delhi
or New York, then that is where the God that I AM –
Physical Form is.

However on a Godly level I am in all places at one time as
I am –
Omniscient
Omnipotent
Omnipresent.

I am not the Baba, Swami, Sai or Lord, you see me to be
in Puttaparthi or elsewhere.
Do not think of me with your Monkey Mind!
I do not have to wear an orange Robe, and am not confined
to a chair!

This Baba, this Sathya, is the ONE I am presenting you
with, to allow you all to experience TRANSITION.
My transition from the Baba you know or saw as a youth,
and the Baba you all see now as an elder of 80 years, and
frail, or so you all most probably think.

THIS FORM is to help you all to realize I will *not* always
be here!
You must all now *think* about going WITHIN to where the
REAL God of all Mankind resides.

I AM THE INDWELLING SPIRIT OF YOUR HEART.
I AM YOU
YOU ARE ME
WE TOGETHER = THE UNIVERSAL 'I'
THE I AM THAT I AM.

YOU
ME
WE
I.

You all only see me during Darshan, Bhajans, in the 'Form'
I present to you at *that* particular time.
I AM FORMLESS – I AM NOT THE FORM.
So better you *adjust* your Monkey Minds from The Form
to The Formless.

Yes my dear well written – a few mistakes – a little
imperfection is fine.
When Baba says 6 kilometres from the Hotel to the
Airport, I mean 6 kilometres not 6 miles. Never question
what I ask you to write please.
As your third book says with so much clarity –
The changing times of old, are soon to be presented with
another option.
Another choice you ask?
Yes my dear, another option or another choice.
You too my dear, still think too much about My Form.
Go deeper still – until you and I become ONE again.

More heart work this evening please, and also do not
forget Your Grid and Liquid Crystal Work!
Much joy and beauty awaits you – if you will surrender
still further to Me.
I am Your Sai.

26.06.06.
6.00 a.m.

Feeling pampered and loved, after an overnight stay yet again at
the Taj in Varanasi. Relaxed and watched Larry King interviewing
Jane Fonda on CNN. What a great interview!

To have seen Jane in 'Klute,' years ago – and then in and with all the publicity surrounding The Vietnam War. Finally to watch with admiration the *true* love between a father and daughter in 'On Golden Pond'.

Apparently she has just released her book – 'My Life so Far.' Many a time during the interview I watched and felt the emotion emanating from deep within her Soul. I laughed when she said she had been celibate for six years – with only a dog for company.
She talked about her childhood, mother, father, and her own life as she purported it to be, including her own family and marriages.

To reach the heights, or let us say pinnacle of life – not unlike Shirley MacLaine, and then realise it took you ALL those years of life or death, to finally realise the Truth of 'Who You Really Are'!

Larry King was an excellent Interviewer, and ever so sensitive and gentle with her. Many a time her eyes would well up with tears, as she spoke about different aspects of her life.
I think she lived at one time in Alabama – in the south of The States – where she activated 'Sexual Equality for Women'.

Yes my dear – Jane is A TRUE ACTIVIST – campaigning for Women's Rights on all levels.
Her abundant and stable upbringing allowed her to BECOME the beauty of 'Who' she really is! However, she was unable to fulfil her *true* potential, as time and time again she gave AWAY her Spiritual Essence, to a Being of *supposed* more power.

She did not understand TRUE power, which her Father had, was a power – an inner power; you are born with and die with.

The Feminine aspect of her Divine Nature was unable to manifest, due to 'associated' problems arising from her Mother's Feminine aspect of Self.

So Jane had amazing opportunities bestowed upon her as a daughter from a Father's perspective, and yet suppressed the qualities that were presented from the Mother's aspect of Self – by and from her own Mother. Why?
Because of Fear!
All 'supposed' suppressions are mainly due to only one aspect of The Divine Nature – FEAR!

Fear of not being good enough.
Fear of rejection from her peers.
Fear of abandonment from her husbands.
Fear of Death of Self – the true and underlying cause of her so-called 'high profile' Social Activation Qualities!

Not so much different to you my dear!
You both had an 'arrhythmia' – an irregular patterning or shadow cast through the left hand side of your DNA – only in sections thank goodness!
The more you distanced yourself from The Spiritual Aspect of Self – THE ONE – the more EXTREME and highly motivated your behaviour became.

THE LESS YOU FELT INSIDE – THE MORE YOU BECAME ON THE OUTSIDE, or so it appeared to those on the outer level of Society – family, friends, peers.
In actual fact, the *more* you died inside, the *more* extreme your behaviour became.
From an 'outsider' looking in – it would appear you both have it all!
In actual fact, you had a 'zero' balance to work from, in regard to 'Who Am I Really?'

This is why emotionally when you realise there is nothing else but God – you actually THEN begin your Spiritual Quest in earnest!

Others – who appear, or are actually more subdued, or quieter in nature, generally do not have the areas of – let us say – Catastrophe – to bring them into the NOW. Remember, out of great hardship and adversity, comes a huge amount of Spiritual Growth and Empowerment – True Empowerment – HOWEVER ONLY IF YOU ARE READY TO SURRENDER, READY TO GIVE, AND READY TO RECEIVE!

Yes I hear you thinking – but Mother Theresa, The Dalai Llama, even Eckhart Tolle, are or were all quieter in nature.
All an illusion my dear – all an illusion.
They all may *appear* quieter in nature, but have an underlying strength that has been activated in times gone by. You do not reach great Spiritual Heights by being or acting – like a Lamb!

So they may have the *appearance* of a quieter nature – but in truth they are strong personalities, determined, just, respectful, compassionate and grateful, however, do not cross swords with them! They have been and still are – IN THE POWER OF NOW!

Om Sai Ram.

So my driver now *thinks* we can make Kedarnath and back to the airport on time, for my Nepal Trip!
How can I not make it – with God on OUR SIDE!
All will be taken care off, this I am sure, however what is the personal and human cost?

A throw away comment a little while ago has slightly unsettled me – 'You only sit in the back and write – whereas we are actually driving!'

The arrogance of the male rearing its ugly head yet once again! Obviously *this* trip for my driver is all about cost – the almighty dollar! It is not really having the Spiritual Significance I thought it would for him – so what is his lesson in this lifetime?

You may well ask!

The lesson is to put God first and foremost, and that 'inner' knowing is to be your guide.

How can God be first when he devalues your Spiritual work, as just a COST he has to bear!

And life will come at a COST for him – wait and see!

So he thinks you sit around and do nothing much, stay at a good hotel, and relax!

Interesting perception to say the least.

When you *attend* to my work – God's work – on a deeper Spiritual and Human level, then what appearances hold true for some on the outside, are not actually TRUTH themselves.

If I require you to be rested, and well nourished, then that is my wish and also my right – AS THE DIVINE.

You do or attend to important work for Baba – Your Lord, then you are *allowed* by the Grace of God, to stay at what I regard as 'appropriate' accommodation.

During your life my dear you have slept on many floors, and eaten incorrectly, as money, home comforts and nourishment, were *not* always available.

You have transcended all of this *now* – and God and the goodness of The Almighty, will transcend into the very Essence of your Being.

Chant the Mantra –
Om Namaha Shivaya
Hara Hara Namaha
Om Namaha Shivaya.

So what you want to know is – do you 'allow' the negative aspect of others to influence and interfere with Your Very Destiny?

You had trials at the beginning of your trip, and trials now, as you are approaching the end of your journey.
Do you change drivers now at Delhi or Agra, and will this in any way lessen, or have a karmic effect on the rest of your journey?

Yes and No.
It was appropriate you 'complete' your old karmic patterns and faults with this driver, as he contains many – let us say qualities, you have been forced into recognizing and tolerating in this particular lifetime.
So your Karma with him will be complete the minute he delivers you to the airport for the remainder of your trip.
Or through necessity if I DEEM IT TO BE – before or after the visit to the last Jyotirlinga.

His suggestion to visit the 12th Jyotirlinga later was completely inappropriate! Not to mention – he was ready to leave on the 1st June, and not at all happy about 6.00a.m. on the 06.06.06. A more auspicious day you could not have chosen – and Ganesha's Day as well!
A Divine Blessing to begin your trip on, no matter what he or anyone else may think.

He minimizes your work because you are a female. If you were a male sitting in the back seat with a briefcase, then his approach to you would have been different.

And yet he has no qualms about asking you for money to help him with his business worries.

You are *not* his keeper!

You are *not* the keeper of any more male influences in your physical life!

If his heart truly shone with the love of God, then he would accept his fate and karma as just that – that it is!

Sink to the bottom as graciously as one can – Mine your own Dark, and rise into the Centeredness of Being – God Centred that is – BY SURRENDERING in totality to every thought, word, action and deed.

Only when you have all surrendered in totality to me – can I THEN give you 'The Key' to help unlock the chains that have bound you all to this life.

Human Life is just what it is – Human.

It is a Godly life you should all strive for – a life full of truth, righteous conduct, peace, love and non-violence.

The 5 Human Values or 'true' Life Qualities, are what you must all strive to attain.

The 5 Human Values are the Mainstay of Humanity or Society here on Earth, if you ALLOW them to play out in the positive aspect of Self – THE I AM THAT I AM.

Wait until this evening, and then we will discuss the remainder of your trip.

Remember, your trip is first and foremost about you – you doing your work at my request, THEN about others, and their agendas.

Bless you my Child.

27.06.06.

The trip from hell.

After yesterday's experience – I must confess to thinking –
'What on Earth am I doing – putting my physical body through
so much stress and duress'?

The trip from Varanasi to Agra took nearly 17 hours! An interlude
of meandering occasionally – away from the main highway –
inadvertently, of course.
Observing quietly the mentality of others.
Why ask an innocent by-stander in a village – the way to Agra?
Why not ask a policeman, driver or motorcyclist?
Why ask a stationary stall keeper, who most probably lives behind
his stall?
I guess it is all that male / female power struggle – the struggle
for and of survival at all and every cost, and let me tell you –
there has been a huge cost *this* particular trip.

The one thing I do not need to hear first thing in the morning is a
conversation of negativity –
'It is too difficult, all too long a trip, or do-able, but you might not
get to the airport on time.'
'If we had left a week earlier!'
'Could you see the last Jyotir Lingam – number 12, on your
return from Mt.Kailash?'
'After all, you are just sitting in the back of the car – we are
actually driving'!

Because of the lateness of the trip, we missed the Agra turnoff,
and then saw, as did the drivers – the sign 190 kms. to Delhi – so
knew Agra was 10 kms. back!
As 10.00p.m. approached, I felt literally ill with exhaustion, lack
of food, and of course dehydration.

Finally into the hotel – a fabulous room, and the best night view of The Taj Mahal from the window. It's a sad feeling to be so tired you feel nauseated with dinner, and no time to relax in the huge bath. A quick wash and into bed for sleep – horizontal rest! Every vein that could have burst from the knees to the ankles had burst! My physical body aching and paining. At nearly 60 years – what on earth am I doing?

Oh yes – The Jyotir Lingam Work for Baba – Shiva – but my physical discomfort, and lateness of arrival in the evening, is preventing me from attending to the *extra* work!

Work, work, my dear – You are doing work and lots of it! You are finally exacting Your Karmic Negative Attraction to ALL Men!
Yes, your driver has many aspects of both previous husbands, however, the second one in particular.
So you are being presented with yet once again the OPPORTUNITY for growth – Personal Growth!

What areas you enquire?
The areas of you having to compromise your standards to accommodate others, and still with inner strength and resolve maintain EQUANIMITY!
So you have learnt to weigh up the personality traits of others that do not reflect YOUR character or ideals – and listen to what I say!

Your Karma will self resolve after *this* trip.
The reason I particularly chose *this* driver for you was because many 'personality' traits have been infused into the cells of his being. Most qualities you have endured and suffered through. You understand what I am saying here!

It is not that his driving skills are not excellent – they are, and he has been good, necessary support for you, at various stages of your journey.
However now, by the end of your 12 Jyotirlinga trip at Kedarnath, you will have paid him back in full – many times over, by compensating and relaxing your boundaries, to learn The True Art of EQUANIMITY.

It is this I need for you to experience one last time before you venture forth into The World and Wilderness.
Do not dwell on the Negative aspect of others. They – your driver in particular, has helped you to discover more of 'Who' You Really Are.

So 'Who' Are You Really, and what have you learnt on THIS Trip?'

1. Equanimity
2. Tolerance
3. Patience
4. Endurance
5. Compromise
6. More Love
7. Abundance
8. Luxury
9. The necessity for Physical Fitness
10. The necessity for correct Nourishment
11. More Trust and Faith
12. Perception
13. Diversity
14. Minimal needs / requirements
15. Empowerment
16. Love of money can be the root of all evil
17. Aloofness and detachment
18. Separation from the expectation of an outcome

19. Who your true friends really are
20. To see the God in ALL
21. To look past The Maya, into The Godliness of True
    Life or Eternal Life.

And these are just a few –
The main areas really are – Truth, Righteous Conduct,
Peace, Love and Non-violence.
THE 5 HUMAN VALUES encompass the Very Essence
of Man.

I am much pleased with you my dear, that is why I prefer
you to rest in luxury, rather than elsewhere.
Please attend to your every need on this trip, as finances
will come to help accommodate this.

Even I smiled when you thought –
'Well if Baba is in charge, of course I can make it!'
'He will just change time or delay the plane!'
I smile at your innocence, however I also smile at your
RESOURCEFULNESS, RESILIANCE AND
BOUNTIFUL COMPASSION.

Yes my dear – a back-up plan from your friend Sunita and
her family, gave you the extra courage and confidence you
required, to help fulfil Your Destiny, as well as the others
connected to you.
To know you can make one call and your friend will
organize the rest of your trip, and another driver at any
time, was indeed *another* blessing.

God bless Sunita – Angelina, and 'Who' is she really?

Driving along – feeling better – all well in God's World.
Hopefully this evening we will reach Haridwar by 6.00 p.m.
Trying to have *no* expectations – great if we can, as my

physicality is really suffering, however understand if we do not.
This then is once again – ALL IN THE DIVINE PLAN.

Thinking also about business – money – in July and now.
Then My Lord said 'Sell everything up NOW' – so I am in the
process of trying to do just that.
Another move to where?

While resting last evening I asked – 'Where is my Soul Mate
Baba?'
And then he was there, 'I am here, right beside you, cannot you
see me yet?'
I feel he is with me on and off.
Even in Varanasi, the thought of being on a boat and seeing all
'The Ghats' was exhausting, and then I knew we would do that
together.
The same feeling with The Taj Mahal in Agra. As I looked out
of the window, and thought about the lack of time to be a tourist
on *this* trip – I knew I would be back later as well!
To actually have the time to see and do an occasional 'tourist'
adventure would indeed be a welcome relief some day.

So what of The Jyotir Lingam work Baba?

No work today my dear.
No work – just remember to ring Amma and Margot –
otherwise NO other work.
Oh yes, access your email before you leave for Tibet as
well.

Om Sai Ram.

You are forever in My Heart, and Your Pain and discomfort
IS My Pain and Discomfort.
Rest my dear, rest and walk a little.

So you are still 'milling' over what I said about – what
your greatest learning and strengths were!
And yes, you are right – The one true strength above all
for you at this stage of Your Spiritual Journey – IS
FORGIVENESS.
You have done well my dear, and yes, this is your TRUE
strength, and will have the total – all encompassing result,
positive result – for yourself, and of course Mankind in
general.

There is no greater or fulfilling action emanating from the
Human Soul and Psyche than THE POWER TO
FORGIVE, and the EMPOWERMENT to do so with love,
grace and compassion.
Top of The Spiritual Class my dear – the top!
You are now graduating from The Sai Kindergarten –
through Secondary College in leaps and bounds.
No, no my dear, not at University yet!

See what happens when you do not react or over react to
problems, and allow them to simmer?
The pot eventually boils over, and what is the outcome?
An empty pot – that is all!
Release your frustrations regarding the maintenance of
your trip, and enjoy my bliss – The Bliss I am indeed
handing you today.
You are a much-blessed child of mine.
Sai – Your Swami.
Your Eternal Love and Friend.

Lingam 12

KEDARNATH
Rudra Prayag, Uttar Pradesh

27.06.06.

LINGAM 12 – KEDARNATH.
Rudra Prayag, Uttar Pradesh.

*After the killing of the Kauravas, the Pandavas felt guilty
for their sins, and meditated on Shiva at Mt. Kailash. After
a long time they found Shiva disguised as a Cow. They
followed the cow to Mt. Kedarnath. Bhima, the strongest of
the Pandavas found the cow and caught hold of its body.
However the front half of the cow disappeared and only the
hind part was left. Shiva was impressed with their devotion,
and both he and Parvathi came to reside at Kedarnath.
Krishna and Arjuna performed intense meditation to Lord
Shiva to stay on the mountain with Parvathi. Their wish was
granted.*

*It is said the fore part of the Cow detached itself and formed
a lingam in Kathmandu, Nepal, and is known as the
Pasupathinath Lingam.*

Well here I am at Gaumukh, the last vehicle stop, before a 14 kilometre hike up the mountain to Kedarnath.

It is a quaint little village – very atmospheric, very hilly, with not too many Westerners, however a few Indian Tourists.

The scenery on the way from Haridwar, through Rishikesh, right into the mountainous terrain, was the best I have seen so far!

I was mesmerised by the great beauty of the huge mountains, covered completely with flora – all varieties of trees and shrubs, too numerous to count.

The landscape was tiered with low stonewalls – a paradise, as far as the eye could see.

Rice fields and corn growing was all I encountered – no cattle, sheep or goats, as per usual in India. However many ponies and mules with saddles – obviously a main mode of transport.

Another 20 kms. further on we passed a 'Helipad' – that really intrigued me. Joy oh joy, a helicopter ride to the top!

A 15 minute ride, instead of a long, uncomfortable trek on a pony, or a 14 km. mountainous walk!

However it was not meant to be! It had not flown for two days because of the bad weather.

Energetically I guess – walking is for the best anyway!

How will my body cope though?

It must be thirty years since I have ridden a horse, and that was only for a few months, and practising 'Dressage' at that!

The little village reminds me of Fall's Creek Ski Lodge in Victoria, Australia, with all verandas facing into each other – a real community and commune type of atmosphere.

So the mountain tomorrow Swami – and The Kedarnath Jyotir Lingam and Temple.

What apparent joy is in store for me?

Well my dear – last, last of your 12 Jyotilingas!
Well done, however definitely a bit of stress and strain on
your physical body tomorrow.
Now listen carefully –

Ride for half an hour and walk for half an hour; then as you
feel better, one hour of walking and riding, if your body
can take the strain.
Remember, the climb will be up hill, and you were short
of breath just walking up three flights of stairs to your
room today!

Also please take some aspirin today as well. We do not
need thrombosis at this late stage – do we?
One aspirin tonight, one in the morning, and one tomorrow
evening, before the long journey home.

Yes, I am smiling – Arab Horses for both you and your
driver because of your size! No, you are not huge, but you
could lose 10 kilos as soon as you arrive home. A minimum
of 10 kilos – as you will already have lost 5 kilos on your
trip to Tibet, as you walk around the base of Mt. Kailash.

Yes, your driver is in good spirits – this is a 'true' holiday
for him, as well as your co-driver.
You ask now about the bells ringing every now and then?
Another blessing, another Puja.

29.06.06.

Up early at 4.30 a.m. and on the Pony Trail by 5.00 a.m.
The small hamlet of Gaumukh, is very much like the villages in
between the Nepal and Tibet border. As usual, no Westerners
anywhere to be seen.

The ride up the mountain was quite stressful. The Ponies doing a remarkable job – but at what cost?
Pony and Arm Chair rides everywhere, not to mention the occasional Sadhu, or local person walking.

Nearer to the top – 14 kms, it was extremely steep!
A woman passed by singing Shiva Bhajans, so I thanked God once more, and prayed more – for the somewhat torturous and dangerous ride to finish successfully.
Stopped briefly to walk about quarter of a kilometre from the top. The air was so thin, I had become breathless.
At one time the young boy looking after our Ponies was very casually walking about four inches from the edge of a ravine.
After a talking to – he became more vigilant, needless to say!
Many offers of help from locals – Puja requirements, etc. and after a brief interview chose the most sincere looking boy.

The scenery on the way up the mountain was unbelievably beautiful. The streams roaring down the mountainside – eventually to form the Ganges.
A delicate mist covering the snow covered peaks of the mountains, lush and green.

Our Lord has patiently waited for the 'Work' to be completed, before allowing the Monsoon to greet us!
My friend Sunita and my drivers all remarking that the season was definitely late – and coincidentally, as we left each particular State, the rain began to pour! Coincidence?

Finally my first viewing of the Temple – such majesty – perched high up on the mountain top.
The driver and I entered The Temple and Jyotir Lingam area with relative ease, as we were walking on the 'wrong' side, to see the Jyotir Lingam.
It was huge and definitely the size of a Buffalo Hump!

I knelt to do my own Puja and pray as I usually do, however the Puja Priest insisted on touching the ghee, flowers and garlands. It was quite disconcerting, and the *first* time this had happened, as usually they just say 'garland,' and I do as I am told by Swami. Probably even more upsetting was the Priest 'splitting' my gifts between the driver and myself!
Baba was *not* happy!
Also the priests were touching my hands!

You cannot 'split' the Energy at the completion of Your Journey!

The Puja completed with my offering of prayers and gifts to Parvathi, and then we left, as it was basically chaos!
As soon as we were outside Baba said –
'Not good enough – You must go back!'
So I coerced the Puja Man with money – and back inside we went – up the wrong side again – to avoid the chaos as best we could, and gain access to the 'inner' sanctum.

Standing directly in front of The Jyotir Lingam again – realizing dollars speak louder than words – and asked the Priest for the 'sacred' milk.
At first the Priest was not overly impressed, especially as the request had come from a woman, however once again – the value of a dollar!

I knelt before the Lingam, and drenched the hindquarter of 'The Hump' with milk.
The energy came through me so powerfully, I couldn't believe it, and neither could a few of the others! A feeling of total spiritual empowerment coursing through my veins.
All in all an amazing experience – to complete the 12 Jyotir Lingams!
Feeling blessed and happy – so headed down to the road to mount the Pony, yet once again!

Dreading the journey downwards, as we had all been told to lean right back in the saddle, because of the steepness. The saddles were not exactly 'padded' either.

Up on to the pony and ready to go. He backed away from the young boy holding the reins, who was to lead us back down the track – another 14 kilometres.

The young boy gave the pony a bit of a 'pat' on the hindquarter, but he would not budge! Then a little more force!

It was then the pony's knees gave way, and he began to fall!

I managed to keep my legs up in the stirrups, as he was brought to his knees – THEN COLLAPSED – not looking very good I must say!

Help!

The young boy could not get him to rise again – so there he lay, for what seemed like ages.

Finally after resting – and making sure the pony had not suffered a heart attack, he managed to get to his feet.

We all agreed to walk *this* pony down the track, and hire another one.

It was all about money again – until I said – 'Pay whatever – to get us down please'!

Whilst walking – by now in *true* agony, my driver mentioned that he thought my energy had been too powerful for the pony.

Yes, I would have to agree!

Especially as I had just experienced monumental surges of Shiva Energy flow through me, after the 2nd Puja.

The journey downwards – well what can I say?

At times we were on a 90 degree angle – and could not even see the pony's head!

The steps were huge, dangerous, slippery, with holes varying from four inches to one foot – here, there, everywhere.

Even whilst on the other pony, Baba would say – 'Stop now and walk for a while.' About three kilometres I tried to walk, the other eleven kilometres ridden in agony.

I prayed to Shiva, Parvathi, Baba, and Amma –
Om Namaha Shivaya, The Gayatri Mantra, The Lord's Prayer, you name it – I performed it.
Without hesitation I can honestly say – it was the most physically exhausting and debilitating trip I have ever experienced.
Of course over the past 18 months – no walking, yoga, or swimming – only God's work!
So what to expect!

Finally after walking the last two kilometres, we arrived back at the village. I could not even remove my track shoes or socks.
My young driver attended to this duty, as all I could do was lie on the bed.
A quick wash then off to sleep – it was only 3.00 p.m.
Well God had another thought about that!

My whole body became extremely sore, and started vibrating and releasing vast amounts of pent up energy!
It became hot, cold, and then went into a kind of exhaustion, a deep cellular shock – that I could NOT control!
Fortunately I had asked my young driver to look in on me every hour – so tried to relax as best I could.

Well, then the tears began – mountains of repressed emotion, came bubbling to the surface. There I was in absolute agony, shivering, and with a down pouring of emotion stronger than I had ever felt before.
'Lifetimes,' Swami said.
'Lie still until 6.00 p.m. at least, before you move.'
It was *so* difficult as my knees, buttocks, and lower back were burning with pain.

At 7.45 p.m. and after a very small bowl of dhal and rice, courtesy of my young driver, I tried to sleep again.

Well Baba – first of all, my poor Pony – what happened?

The pure Energy of The Divine, surged through your entire Physicality – every cell, every atom, also the 'Trident' Energy of Shiva ran through your spine.
We will discuss this all tomorrow, as now you have to rest.
The two horses from today will leave the animal kingdom and incarnate as humans – in their next life
A Divine Blessing today was bestowed upon them both.
The Pony you could not ride down, and the one you actually rode down.
Their Karma is now complete – they will leave their Earthly Bodies soon.
Yes, I see you thinking – not that much different to Amma's favourite Cow – yes, you may expand on your story.
More water please!

Om Sai Ram.

Last year after arriving in Bangalore from Australia, we were driving towards Puttaparthi.
About two hours into the journey a strong feeling came over me, and then I was told in no uncertain terms, to turn around and drive 6 hours south to Mysore to visit The Divine Mother.

I questioned this, however the voice of God was absolutely certain –
'Go to Mysore and drink the 'special' milk from the Cow!'
Not quite understanding what the statement meant I quickly made a phone call – only to be told that very morning Amma's favourite Cow had given birth to a calf.
It was then I asked the driver to turn the car around.

After the necessary formalities, Amma presented me with a bowl of special dessert that she had made – like baked custard – very rich and creamy. This 'dessert' was made from the first milk produced after the birth of the calf – I guess like 'colostrum' – the first milk from the mother to the babe. It was very tasty and very sweet, not to mention extremely nutritious!

Early the following morning I drove to the Spiritual Centre to visit the cow and newly born calf.
The calf was so beautiful and looking ever so divine, as I stroked her nose.
I looked into the cow's big brown eyes and thanked her for the glorious dessert I had partaken of the evening before, and left, for the eight-hour journey north.

Upon nearing almost the exact position we had turned around the day before, the phone rang. It was a call from a friend from the Centre.
'Amma's favourite Cow has just had a heart attack and died!'
'Do not ring Amma, as she is still too upset to talk to anyone.'
Stunned, I prayed and felt really bewildered, as I had visited the cow that morning!

On and on we drove, and then I thought to ask what had happened, as the sadness was overwhelming.
The voice was firm and clear –

'Better the Cow than YOU!'

Then I remembered my family history, with heart attacks and high cholesterol.
A very sad day for Amma's Cow, and a reprieve for Yours Truly.

9.40 p.m.

Up early again – ready to leave by 5.30 a.m. – down the mountain.

The Monsoon rains have already begun!

It's interesting – the rain first began to drizzle on the way up the mountain yesterday. It was wonderful to see the many different coloured raincoats, dotted here and there over the mountainside.

Yes for sure – the Monsoon is here!

What joy – I love the rain, and my aching body is feeling a little better after the rest.

Landslide after landslide, dirt, rubble, rocks and huge boulders! The bulldozers are out in full force, as well as many helpers – trying to clear the road.

In two evenings and one day the weather has changed dramatically.

Now clouds are covering the top – peak of the mountains.

It's an eerie feeling being in a 'Void of Mist.'

We encountered many accidents on the way down the mountain.

Trucks and cars here and there, either upended or just stationary, from the wet and slippery roads.

Reminiscing about my Childhood.

I remember so clearly asking my father to drive faster on the winding roads. He always drove slowly, almost excruciatingly so, not that much different to my driver now.

Then a few kilometres further down the road, we would see the same cars that had passed, pulled over to the side of the road, for one reason or another.

Oh yes, today children were hanging out of the car windows vomiting, as they were travelling along.

Still thinking about my 'sore' back and the Ponies.

Oh, what Karma!

This evening we are safely back in Haridwar, then on to Delhi tomorrow evening for the last night, before the onslaught of Nepal and Tibet.

The Kedarnath Jyotir Lingam.
A Lingam like no other – the hind section of The Buffalo, or so the story goes.
This is not exactly correct!
The Jyotirlinga at Kedarnath has more to do with 'Lanka' than the Buffalo.
Yes, yes, the story is partially correct, however slightly distorted over eons of time.

Deep within The Heartbeat of India lies a 'hollow' Drum.
Hollow – you ask?
Yes hollow, I say!
For years upon years, the peoples of Bharat have tried to maintain their Spiritual Existence under the most horrific and gruelling circumstances.
They came to Earth, they conquered THEIR land, or so they thought.
No, completely untrue!
The Indian peoples cannot conquer their own land, unless it is given back to them.

From the days of Rama – the days of Rameshwaram – the final point before Lanka, a Spiritual Battle took place. The Divines were outnumbered by the 'Darker' Forces, so all was not quite as it seemed to be.

Yes, yes, Shiva was there, and The Pandavas all arrived to ask Shiva for Forgiveness for the sins they committed against Humanity – sins of the flesh, death and destruction. Yes, they did search and search for Shiva to ask

forgiveness, this is all true – and they were ultimately forgiven because of their persistency.

However, the real reason Kedarnath was such a 'Sacred' place, was its nearness to Holy Mount Kailash and Heaven, or so all thought.

The Energy from Kedarnath has been disjointed and dismantled, since the days of Rama, since he was a frequent visitor to Kedarnath.

This is the actual birthplace of Shiva, or so you may have heard.

The 'hump' always reminded Rama of Lanka and Sita – so he declared this a Holy place, as well as The Jyotirlinga being present there.

However the Energy of the Negative Influences since that time have NEVER totally cleared. In actual fact – the Energy was corrupt!

Yesterday you came along and nonchantly unblocked or cleared the Energy Fields, Grids, Paths, and Rites of Passage as well.

On completion of 'the Clearing' and your 2nd Puja, the PURE Shiva Energy became SO potent, even a Pony or Mule could not stand.

Can you imagine the change to Humanity!

You have cleared a pathway for the Energy now from the 'true' south – Rameshwar Jyotirlinga, to the 'true' north – Kedarnath Jyotirlinga.

You ask 'What does it look like through the 3rd Eye?'

It looks exactly like a Fish – The Infinity Symbol, no less!

A fish capable of facing the four directions –

1. Left handed Guardian – True West
2. True South

3. **True North**
4. **Right handed Guardian – True East.**

**Sleep on this, and then we will talk – also go into your
Crystal Grid for 22 seconds as well.
God Bless You My Child.**

01.07.06.

Well here I am on the way back to Delhi.
Rest and more rest last night – the physical body still aching, and
also looking exhausted as well.
I'm still thinking about The Kedarnath Jyotir Lingam.

**Yes my dear – Your Kedarnath Jyotirlinga.
The Energy from the North to the South Axial 'Graft' Pole.
Rameshwar Jyotirlinga was the 'access' pathway to The
Northern Gate – however not The Northern Gate to India,
but The Northern Gate to Lanka.
And yes, you my dear are Keeper of this Gate as well.
Yes as in your other book – Keeper of The Northern Gate.
So is it Lanka or is it India?
You are a Keeper of The Gateway to Heaven.
The Gateway at Rameshwaram is the southern end of the
Energetic Axis.
Kedarnath is northern most end of the Energetic Axial
Pole or line.**

**The Energy of Kedarnath ties all of the Energy of the other
11 Lingams together.
So to 'exact' your fate, or the fate of Humanity, you
dislodged the congestion, long overdue I might add, and
began to clear the Energetic Axial Pole from Rameshwaram
in the south. You 'pulled' the Energy through and
downwards there.**

Then as you travelled north in sequence, your sequence, you cleared the decongestion, realigned the Energy, and reconstituted the new 'Energetic Waves of Transmission,' or let us say – allowed the 'positive' Energy from The Mother Earth, to once again flow in abundance.

It is as you KNOW it to be – tying up, or lacing up a shoe! First you put the lace in at the top of the shoe, and then pull it through to the bottom, and then you begin to 'lace' up the shoe.
The laces are tied in a criss-cross fashion, all the way up the shoe, and then finally tie at the top, with a criss-cross action.

The 12 Jyotirlinga Energies are permanently tied together as ONE – at this time.
However this is NOT complete for Humanity – Energetic completion that is, for the total good of Mankind.
This *only* occurs when 'The Bow' of the lace is tied, and this *only* occurs after walking around the base of Mt. Kailash.

THEN AND ONLY THEN THE ENERGY WILL BE COMPLETE!
UNITY IN DIVERSITY WILL SOON OR NOW BECOME UNITY IN DIVINTY!

OM SHANKARA OM OM.
OM SHIVA SHANKARA
OM SHIVA SHAMBO
OM OM OM.

So my dear, feeling pleased and happy now – work well done, and very soon to be released in the Form of another NEW book.
All is as it is meant to be.

My love for you is never ending and everlasting!
Om Shanti Om.

6.32 a.m.

Your driver has just been informed The Omkareshwara
Jyotirlinga has cracked!
And you smile and say – Oh I wonder why?'
Smarty Pants are you not?
This is one of your humorous sayings – is it not?
Yes my dear, work very well done – Baba is very happy
with you!
Many, many blessings, are coming your way – many!

The energy of The Omkareshwara Jyotirlinga – the news
on TV said it has cracked – Yes this is truth!
As The Shiva work increases globally, then the Energetic
lines and distribution points and factors change
dramatically.
So naturally there will be vast amounts of 'imbalance' and
negative releases, as The Mother Earth Energy surges
through The 12 Jyotirlingas.

These 12 Lingams in particular, are the main Points, Major
Pathways or Minor Gateways – for the Energetic
Transference of The Earth's Evolution – in ALL Universes
AT THIS TIME!

One Change – No.1 – Rameshwar – must have an effect,
then you link in the other Jyotirlingas, as you travel north.
So after each visit, yet *more* Negative Energy is being
released or cleared.

The TRUE Shiva Energy has been blocked since time
immemorial.

Now by releasing the Positive Energy from The Mother –
The Divine Goddess Energy, then TRUTH &
RIGHTEOUSNESS WILL REIGN SUPREME.

Om Shiva Namaha Om.

You enquire – but many have been visiting The Shiva
Jyotirlingas for a long time. Has the energy always been
blocked?
No, not always, however as The Mother Earth Energy was
nullified, she transmuted her Divine Energy into a 'Slumber
land' of misappropriation of thought, word and deed!
It is just how it is – Mother Earth Energy has to be able to
'move' to help heal Humanity on your Earth, and other
levels of Consciousness.

Through 'misappropriation' – originally from Dark Forces,
The TRUE Shiva Energy first of all stagnated, then
solidified into clumps or patches.
This caused varying degrees of congestion in all Energetic,
everyday Transference Procedures!

So The Shiva Energy becomes a blockage – then Mother
Earth Energy CANNOT MOVE!
ENERGY IS TRANSIENT.
IT IS A CURRENT – IT FLOWS.
SO SHIVA ENERGY BLOCKED
MOTHER ENERGY BLOCKED.

After all Shiva / Mother = ONE!
Are not God / Goddess ONE?
I think so!

Om Namaha Shivaya
Om Shanti Om.

Once again – let me clarify this for your readers, as the way in which I explain to you, is quite convoluted for the average person.

The Shiva Energy has been blocked for a long period of time. The Energy therefore became distorted, and the energetic Pathways became 'Negative' in balance and effect.
This caused the Mother Earth Energy to compound and recompound, until the congestion caused major tidal and Earth shifts. For Example – volcanic eruptions, tsunamis, tidal waves, hurricanes, flooding, holes in the Ozone Layer etc.,
So Male Energy blocked –
Feminine / Mother Earth Energy blocked –
Remember – ALL IS ONE.

New Pathways and Minor Gateways will open automatically NOW.
The Energy of Shiva and The Mother Earth – WILL NOW HEAL THE UNIVERSE!

Om Hari Om.

SOON PEACE AND LOVE WILL REIGN SUPREME!

Om Hara Hara
Om Sai Ram
Om Shiva Shambo
Om Shanti Om.

WELL DONE MY DEAR!

9.45a.m.

So my friend, my dear friend, what have you learnt?

143

You have learnt or rather observed much, however Your
Focus was and still is not – at its peak as yet!
You came
You saw
You conquered?

No!
You did not come – you had already arrived!
You only saw what I intended for you to see at ALL times,
and you have seen ALL.
You did not conquer – as you had already conquered –
Conquered in many lifetimes past.

So what you are asking now is – Has *this* work in *this*
lifetime been done for the good and upliftment of Humanity
or The Earth, at this time in History?

Yes, this time in history, and simultaneous times in other
Realms in other Universes – at this time.

My Friend, my friend – you are, and have never been any
more than a clear Vessel – a clear Channel – to allow MY
WORK, MY ENERGY, MY LOVE to flow through you at
this time in The Universe, and other times in other
Universes.
Remember my dear – ALL IS ONE.

ALL IS ONE
ALL HAS BEEN ONE
ALL WILL BE ONE
ONE IS ALL THERE IS
I AM STILL THAT I AM
I AM THAT
I AM I
I.

144

The lessons learnt during your trip with the two drivers –
have been many and varied!
Yes, I chose them both very carefully for you, to maximise
and optimise your catharses.
You came, You saw, You conquered?
No!
I came, I saw, I conquered!
Swami always has – and always will.
That is my Divine Right and Divine Ordination.

It is nothing other than the WILL OF GOD that has carried
you through.
Many a time it was Your Will – Ego, however as the days
progressed, I managed to subdue and annihilate Your Ego.

The Ego lies in tatters – shreds.
Now you can really begin your work in earnest for Me.
All will only 'now' be forth coming.

Yes, Yes, about time you say.
Yes, this is so.
A little late coming to the Door of Heaven, however better
late than never.

You are my love – true love, and still you do not know –
'Who' You Really Are!
Yes, yes, – Love, God – All there is.
I mean – Who are you Really?
A little mystery to intrigue the senses my dear.
One day, when the timing is right –
ALL WILL BE REVEALED.

You ask about Amma?
Let her be.
She understands and knows the error of her ways, as well
as yours.

Come to me after Mt. Kailash, for three Darshans.
Your Shiva and Parvathi Work completes on the 11th July,
2006.
Yes, I smile – Guru Pournima, and how appropriate!

Do not be too hard on your driver – I chose him – NOT
YOU!
Besides, think of all the lessons and opportunities for
growth!
Well done, and yes, you at long last are smiling too!

Take rest now, and relax, and observe the 'free' flowing
Energy of all the Jyotirlingas.
Years and years of corrupt Energy, and NOW all energy
lines *nearly* flowing to capacity – for THIS time.
Yes, the energy looks to flow freely, however much is still
in a period of transition. So it has the appearance of 'free'
flow, but this will occur spasmodically only – until you
complete your book on the 11th July 2006, then you will
really see – FREE FLOW ENERGY!

This 'free flow' Energy will activate ALL Chakras as well,
so a healing for The Earth and Atmosphere, of course
transcends the bounds of Humanity!
So from the *apparent* lowest of Plant, Animal and Human
Evolution, comes the magnificence and beauty of –
'WHO' ALL REALLY ARE!

The Shiva Jyotirlinga Work over the past twenty-four days,
will change the Energetic and Dharmic Pattern of
Existence.
I will speak to you personally later, about other areas of
life.

Om Sai Ram.

MT. KAILASH
&
MANASAROVAR YATRA

*From the advent of Hindu Religion for the last 5000 years,
it is believed that the sacred rivers originate from the centre
of the Universe, which is Mt. Kailash and Manasarovar.
Mt. Kailash also known as Sumeru Prabat, is the home of
Lord Shiva, and indeed the Indus, Sutlej, Ganges via Karnali,
and the Brahmaputra Rivers, begin at this most holy spot.
Not only is Mt. Kailash important for Hindus, but for
Buddhists, Jains and Sri Sathya Sai Baba followers as well.*

*Mt. Kailash is 23,080 feet above sea level, and is a snow
covered rock pyramid. It is located in the scenically rich
area of Western Tibet. It lies between the Himalayan Ranges,
Karakorum Ranges and Mt. Naga; the three great mountain
ranges of Asia. From here one can see into Afghanistan,
Pakistan, India and Nepal. It is often referred to as the
mountain of 'Swastika,' an ancient sign of good luck.*

*It is considered most auspicious to make a Religious
Pilgrimage – Yatra – around the 52 kilometre circuit, or base
of the mountain. In fact the entire region of Mt. Kailash is of
important religious significance, and includes the two*

turquoise blue high lakes of Manasarovar (positive energy) and Rakshas Tal (negative energy).

This holy region is the symbol of creation of the Universe, attracting scholars and researchers worldwide.
Mt. Kailash being the centre of the Himalayas and home of Lord Shiva, provides us with all source of life, and welcomes you to spiritually enriching and rewarding opportunities of a lifetime.

It is said a single ambulation around Mt. Kailash wipes away the sins of a lifetime.

02.07.06.

DELHI:

Well here I am, relaxed, massaged, pampered, nourished, and ready for Nepal and Tibet – Mt.Kailash.

We left Haridwar at 5.30 a.m. arriving in Delhi at 1.30 p.m. All in all a good trip.

Thinking about life and the animals.
Throughout the whole of India, there were mainly cows, bulls and goats. Occasionally a couple of sheep, bullocks, mules, for working, or as a mode of transportation. An occasional group of camels, and two peacocks, and oh yes, a few chickens here and there. Many tiny squirrels scampering up the trees, and quite a few cheeky monkeys.

The terrain from the South – hilly – with reasonably green vegetation.
A huge desert spans the middle of India, with high mountain ranges – red dust everywhere – at other times the terrain a depressing shade of grey!

High up into the North – great beauty and majesty – like I have never seen before.

The Himalayas are truly Nature's Wonder.

Winding roads – terrible at times, however the vegetation very lush, with huge mountain gorges, which were breathtaking.

The River Ganges – a tribute to all – The 'Mother' of India.

Arrived safely at The Taj Palace Hotel in Delhi. Great room, with an uninterrupted view across acres of green treetops. At present I'm looking downwards to the green lawn, flowers, and glistening blue pool below.

The staff were ever so welcoming, and the food – what can I say!

However the best part for me, considering my few days of really having to 'rough it'– was a massage – to relieve the sore, aching body. It was the ultimate massage I have ever experienced.

Thinking about the 12 Jyotir Lingams, and already have begun 'tying-up' the energies together. I have been told to wait until Mt. Kailash, and the final 'tying-up' on the 11th July 2006. Until this time all will *not* be complete energetically. I now know it is likened to tying up your shoe laces – and *not* tying the bow or knot!

Also thinking about another incident – what a drama!

In the Western World you give a quote and that is that, whereas in India, I find the 'money' thing – let us say *more* flexible!

You agree to pay for a 'service' and may have to pay extra because of *other* circumstances, however would it be too much to ask for a few positive comments – Great trip, I learnt a lot, it was amazing seeing so much of India, wasn't that a hair raising adventure! Apparently not – It was all too tiring, not enough money, wrong starting time, etc.

I have looked at my life and life choices – past and present, and have only this to now say – Thank you God for sending me someone who would *definitely* press any old buttons, and bring the *last* remnants of 'old' agendas – mostly relationships – husbands, father – past life and present life – to look at!
I mean – let it go!
Baba – you really did a great job!

All in all, an amazing trip, and the main thing I have learnt is – I still have to remember I DO NOTHING – GOD DOES ALL! Also to Surrender – send more love to all – and finally to practice FORGIVENESS.
Oh yes – and keep My Ego in check – naughty thing it is!

Nearly ready for the airport – the two drivers half way to Mumbai by now, then on to Bangalore.
Leaving soon to meet the Bangalore Mt. Kailash Group, inside The Delhi International Terminal.
Let us see where this part of my trip takes me!

2.20 p.m.

KATHMANDU – NEPAL:

Well here I am on the plane to Kathmandu with forty-nine Indian Nationals. Apparently the other ten from the States will join us in Kathmandu, making about eighty including staff.
So Swami – this is interesting – no Westerners – or as the others would say – no Foreigners!

A mixed array of Merchants, Academics, and their wives – all wearing saris – no less, a few young single men – in good shape. Even the young women look fit!

Waited for our Tour Guide or Leader to appear. Finally he found me – not too hard to find! His name is 'Prasad'.

Prasad – I guess in the form of a Divine Blessing or Gift from God. Even in the airport, the lounge attendant spoke good English, and offered to help me find my group, even though I was not in the lounge!
His name was Kailash!
So all well in God's Land – we are nearly there!

04.07.06.

I was given a tin of 'special' sweets from a friend – a present from Baba, and was told to eat them when it felt appropriate.

Sweet 1:

The purity of love and newness of Spirit abounds in you my dear. You are much Loved and much Blessed.

Yesterday – a day of exhaustion as we packed all of our belongings into a duffle bag, supplied by the Tour Company.
I reluctantly purchased new winter clothes, as my own thermal clothing and winter garments were in storage, somewhere at home.

A friendly and chatty group at breakfast – all excited about their 'own' Spiritual sojourn to Tibet – Mt. Kailash. A Pilgrimage for them ALL! So the love of God shines within us all.

The Hotel stay in Kathmandu, brief and fairly comfortable. I felt truly exhausted after the shopping expedition, then after lifting my duffle bag, experienced severe pain in my lower back, inguinal area, and the outside of my left knee – excruciating pain actually!

Rose at 3.15 a.m. and ready to leave by 4.00 a.m. over the glorious mountain scenery, into Tibet.
Three buses accommodating the sixty of us, plus the staff, helpers and drivers in other vehicles.
All fine, even though I am still aching.

My new friend Maj and I sat together and chatted most of the way to the border. He explained how to grow coffee, rice, cardamom, and black pepper. He also talked about his family – they way in which they lived etc., so even though I had limited understanding of the Coffee Plantation Industry, I found it all very enlightening! Maj is a very knowledgeable, extremely interesting, forty-four year old bachelor.

After a brief stop for lunch and more glorious scenery, we finally left our bus at the Friendship Bridge – the Gateway between Nepal and Tibet.
Encountered the 'usual' passport drama, then over the Friendship Bridge to find a waiting land cruisers or four-wheel drive vehicle.
I must admit – our group – the three single men, Sherpa, driver and myself, made an interesting six!
A coffee plantation owner Maj aged 44 years, Vivek, a Bangalore lawyer – 32 years, and another 32 year old private enterprise young man – working in the family business, somewhere south of Bangalore, and not too far from Maj.

Finally – after much deliberation we found a vehicle – not previously arranged, as we had anticipated! However any 'port in a storm,' as the rain had begun in earnest! Eventually our small group settled in the truck – myself and Tibetan driver in the front – thank goodness, as there was more legroom for my knee and aching calf. The three boys in the back seat, and the Sherpa right in the back with the luggage.

The scenery similar to Kodaikanal in the south of India, and Rishikesh area in the north.
Enjoyed a few laughs here and there – the boys speak their own language, and then communicate with me in English.

Settled into our accommodation for the night – a small guesthouse sleeping 3-4 per room.

Our vehicle was the first to arrive, so already I am in the ladies dormitory, feeling fine.

After the Chinese checkpoint, I met a Research Scientist from the Midwest of the USA. A very interesting and quite humorous woman! She is working in the field of Cancer Research, and her husband in the area of Alzheimer's Research.

So my day is coming to a close Swami – my body feels exhausted and is aching badly. Are there any messages for me?

Yes my dear, clear yourself of, and from the energy of Nepal, Kathmandu – and your shopping expedition.
The Energy of Kathmandu – Nepal, in general, is in huge transition because of the Political and Social pressures brought to bear.
Governments come and go –
The only security you all have –
The one sure thing as you would say my dear –
Is that God stays and dwells in the Hearts of all!

Om Shanti Om
Om Sai Ram
Om Shanti Om.

Rest for one hour now.

05.07.06.

Another day, another lesson.
The extra kilos of body weight I now carry compared to 1997, have certainly changed my body biorhythms and dynamics.

An aching lower back, thighs and knees, from lifting the bags, and a little 'pitting' oedema of the ankles. Also a slight headache and shortness of breath, because of the altitude – about 3700 metres. These symptoms are even affecting *some* in the group, who are *reasonably* fit and healthy.

So drink more water.
Legs up when not walking.
Breathe deeply.
More salt.
Rest, and still more rest.

Whilst attending to The Lingam Work, it was as though I had 'specific' work to attend to daily. Here it is as though it is just a holiday – and showing me the unhealthy balance of my physicality.

We are definitely in Tibet now – the starkness – the bleakness – only a very few patches of greenery here and there. Apparently from tomorrow onwards we will be camping, in sheer isolation from others and home comforts!

This message was given to the wife of the Research Scientist regarding Alzheimer's Disease.

Regarding the Disease –
It is an inherent 'base' gene.
It has a square root of 9.
A Molecular Distribution Ratio or Factor of 3.
An Atomic Mass Proportionate Rate / System of 44 – however very unstable due to Cosmic shifts in the Energies, Frequencies and Vibrations at this stage, so varies from 44-41.
However, all will stabilize by 11th-17th Sept. 2006.

All is as it should be.

Everyone quite friendly, and trying to speak English, as my Hindi is non-existent.

The Energy of Tibet at this moment has a meltdown factor. Yes my dear, yourself and many others *are* suffering.

Be aware – a fool and his money *can* be parted forever.

Janice is not well at home. Send more love to Hildegard, abusive thoughts are presenting in Yvette. Michelle is on her own journey, and not to be asked to help you at this stage. Claire still suffering, as well as the multitudes who 'think' they have all surrendered, when in fact they are surrendering to 'The Darker' Aspect of Me – The Anti Christ!
So be aware, I come in MANY Forms to help Humanity – LIGHT AND DARK – All or Both, will activate change, huge change.

The Energy of Tibet has changed since the British left Hong Kong. The pure, true blood of the Chinese Citizen is becoming absolute in its intent.
To do harm you ask?
No, not necessarily, but to control the World as you know it to be?
Yes, this is a God's Truth!

All of you out there who 'think' you are in charge, and in power – actually are NOT!
The Chinese are the most powerful citizens, and China the most powerful country in the World, at this time.
You are all so busy worrying about the Moslem uprising – you are forgetting where the 'real' uprising is occurring.

Now let us talk about your Lingams –
Just tighten the lace or energy line a little NOW.
Remember – each time you adjust or tighten the lace –
the Energy of India becomes more pure. In most cases –
Purity Reigns Supreme!

However be aware of the 'Dark Forces' that do not want
this to happen.
Remember Light or Dark – all are in Great Gross Fear at
this time on Earth.

Rest your body, and *now* would be a good time to go into
your Liquid Crystal Network and *see* what transpires.
Drink *more* water and elevate your legs – that is all for
now.

Om Sai Ram.

Sweet 2:

**Truth will always be your constant companion – no matter
what eventuates – just Truth!
No more – no less.**

Om Sai Ram.

6.37 p.m.

One would have to ask?
Am I going to make it?
Already someone has gone home.
Some of the group look to be in worse shape than I am in – so let
us see what is in store!
Remembering with fond memories my first trip to Tibet in 1997,
and my friend Janice.

So what has happened this trip?

Well first of all this time we did *not* fly into Lhasa and then acclimatize in the Yarlung Valley. Instead we drove overland straight into the bleak rough areas – not really a sight seeing mission. Also, previously we travelled overland *towards* Nepal, so ended our journey in lush surrounds, with joy and humour.

So is this trip different for me because everyone is Hindu?

I guess so!

There is a huge area of isolation, and yet everyone is trying to be friendly.

The 'unattached' tend to band together as usual – the married couples always more self contained and content, just with each other.

So am I feeling alone – powerful, or lonely – a sad and sorry state of destitution?

On the previous trip into Tibet I thoroughly enjoyed the company of Janice, Hildegard, Lizzie, David – all seemed to flow.

My dear, dear, friend.

So you weep tears of sadness for yourself – or are they Soul Tears – for a life you have *not* attained as yet?

Is there still an expectancy or expectation in regard to Your Life?

I think so!

Just rest for one hour, and do your Crystal Grid Work, then we will talk.

Om Sai Ram.

9.40 p.m.

Well here I am after a glorious dinner, however the curry is causing my body a bit of grief!

In bed already, and ready to rise early by IST – Indian Standard Time or is it Indian Stretchable Time?

A brief stop at the email shop – the last one before 'The Coup!' The boys happy after a few local drinks – so all well.

Looking forward to tomorrow, however now realise the 'gloss' of the trip to Tibet, has been lost temporarily. I guess because I have driven some of the route before.

The whole group are now talking to me, smiling, making sure I am all right, even the cooks and helpers.

Just relax my dear, you are so accustomed to 'actual' working, you feel uncomfortable just resting! For years you have worked on all and many levels, and now you are to rest, and I will help you cross over the void into a World of Bliss and Dreams.

Your new friend's husband cannot isolate the 'exact' proportion of the gene that causes the Alzheimer's disease, because he is still not actually looking at the correct section. Nearly there – but not quite though.

LINGAM PROGRESSION WORK:

Now let us look at the Progression on The Lingam Work:

Lingam 1 – Rameshwar.
The energy is now in 'full' throttle, and many are experiencing their worst nightmares, as a deep, deep, cleansing occurs.

Lingam 2 – Srisailam – Mallikarjuna.
More moderate energetically – more balanced and calming.

Lingam 3 – Bhimashankar.
Acute depressive feelings will arise, within those who 'touch' the Lingam over the next six weeks to six months.

The Energy has shifted and is now clearing – a deep cleansing from The Mother, is now in place.

Lingam 4 – Grishneshwar.
Return to Mother Earth in all her Glory.
Those who visit *this* Lingam will feel the need to surrender to The Mother. Huge waves of compassion are emanating from this Lingam at this time.

Lingam 5 – Tryambakeshwar.
Sorrow, deep sorrow. Many will experience an Energy of transition, as the Energy Channels open, and perfect their mission of Energetic and Magnetic Exchange.

Lingam 6 – Omkareshwar.
Areas of convoluted Energy have not cleared adequately at this time, causing areas of panic and confusion to arise within many.

Lingam 7 – Mahakaleshwar.
As the mountains fret and the tides change, so will the face of this particular Lingam. The 'pull' of The Earth will cause minor areas of calamity, for a period of time yet.

Lingam 8 – Nageshwar.
The Energy of the sea will impact on the clarity, structure and expansion of The Universe, in direct alignment with the Energy of Mother Earth.

Lingam 9 – Somnath.
To be or not to be?
Yes, that is definitely the answer to the Divine Question.

Lingam 10 – Vishwanath.
Pure truth, pure beauty, is emanating forth in all directions. The clearing of The Earth is propelling forth at this time.

Lingam 11 – Vaidyanath.
Deep, deep, sorrow and resentment is being released globally, as the Energy of this particular Lingam reconstitutes its rightful position once more – within the elements of change.

Lingam 12 – Kedarnath.
The route may be difficult, the area may be tortuous at times, however the Energy of the final Lingam is now 'tying together' the Energy of the other 11 Lingams. This will create and cause Global / Universal and Cosmic Change at THIS time.
Ultimately all for the good of Mankind.
Om Sai Ram.

07.07.06.

Sweet 3 –

Resemblance and Disorder.
Resemblance of what – you may ask?
Resemblance of God Almighty – Your Lord – THE I AM THAT I AM.

Disorder – When you lose the total ability to BE AT ONE WITH ME – because of the Disorder and Disarray in your Life, thus causing a 'Domino' effect on others.
You must retain and remain in total order. Another way of saying 'disorder' would be to say – LOSS OF FOCUS!
Chaos, disorder – all lead to 'loss' of Focus!
Loss of Focus leads to your retaining your personality / thoughts / agendas – THE I – THE EGO – Not Divine Will – Your Will!
Who will win?
Not You I assure You.
Om Sai Ram.

Another day passed.
We are now on the way to Lake Manasarovar and Holy Mt. Kailash.
Let me retrace my steps – from yesterday.
Well let me put it this way – I have experienced some fairly horrific times in my life – but nothing could compare to yesterday.

Up early, and all seemingly fine.
A quick breakfast, then off for another day of adventure.
The road was without a doubt the worst I had ever travelled.
Not actually a road, just dirt, dust and corrugations.
The conditions were unparallel to any road I have ever driven on. We all agreed on that score!

As the day progressed, my eyes and legs became very oedematous, followed by a blinding headache, with blurred vision, aching back of neck, and a mild rash.
Then the nausea and vomiting began!
I prayed to be taken – as the rigors and sweating overtook my body.
To make matters worse, I was with five others who were *equally* debilitated!
The accommodation was filthy, and the toilets – well you could *not* imagine!

We were all visited by the lovely Dr. Prasad a couple of times.
He was kept *very* busy!
BP fine, thank goodness. He suggested 'Diamox' immediately – for thinning the blood, and anti-nausea tablets, however soon they were all floating in the bowl as well.

I remembered briefly a time in Egypt, with my friend Janice, when the Energy of the Great Pyramid overtook me – the nausea and dizziness – and wanting to die ! Somehow *this* felt worse – and of course no friend for support either!

An interesting night!

Now we are again in the vehicle to continue our journey. Thought briefly about hiring a Helicopter, and to ring Sunita. Then remembered it would be difficult with Chinese / Nepalese Customs!

We are all feeling marginally better – usually the boys are a bit of fun – sitting in the back chatting in Hindi – so it gives me plenty of time to think and pray!

However, with the unbelievable condition of the roads, I'm more intent on trying to protect my back and knees.

So today I felt 100% better than yesterday, however on a scale of 1-10 – about a 3!

Finally we arrived at our overnight stop.

We are totally in the Nederlands of Tibet.

The accommodation – well at least it may be antiquated, however the rooms are reasonably clean.

No bathrooms or toilets, just two holes in the ground – which is already a problem, as the holes are only 2 feet long and 9 inches wide!

Fortunately after a bit of pressure, I have a room on my own. The only problem being, the main compressor for the whole area is in this room. No wonder no-one wanted to share!

Let us see what eventuates when the lights go on later!

I feel protected energetically – so all fine.

Tomorrow we arrive at 'Manasarovar' for a spot of camping.

I quite like the idea of a tent, besides, in Kathmandu I purchased my own sleeping bag. To be at peace and in one place for a few days, will be a blessing indeed!

The terrain in this part of Tibet – China – is even more rugged and isolated than I can remember. Miles upon miles of 'unforgiving' land. Huge bleak brown mountains and sand dunes.

Plateaus of desert, with occasional patches of green scrub. Framing this plateau are the snow-capped peaks of The Himalayas as well. The sky is the most glorious deep blue – the clouds pure white – not patches of drifting clouds we see at home.

The children appear to be more aggressive than nine years ago. They hold out their hands – with absolute expectation, so I gave freely the toothbrushes and combs I had with me. Later on, an older boy came by and motioned he also wanted a comb and toothbrush. I offered him a pen instead – he was not happy, and gave me a filthy look.

I guess when tourists give – it sets precedence for all – so basically the root of another self-perpetuating problem.

The fellow members on the trip are ever so friendly, and talk to me now.

Oh yes, about half way up the mountain pass, the vehicle in front of us stopped, and the driver jumped out to place a stone under the wheel. As he was searching for the stone, the vehicle began to roll backwards.

The look on the faces of the five trapped inside was something I will never forget in a hurry, as the vehicle rolled over the edge of the mountain and plunged downwards.

We all jumped out of our vehicle – just in time to see it come to rest in a small ravine! There it balanced in the most precarious position – about 60-70 feet down. Eventually all were helped out of the vehicle, and struggled to the top of the cliff, and on to the road.

After some First Aid – as all were in varying degrees of shock, checking of limbs, and covering to keep warm – all settled – resting on the side of the mountain. The whole road was blocked by now, with many vehicles all wanting to help – one way or another.

Down the mountainside went twenty or thirty drivers and Sherpas, placing rocks under the wheels to prevent the vehicle sliding into infinity! Then steel cables were placed around the 'high' side of the vehicle for strength and stability.
Much pushing, pulling, and motor checking ensued.
Finally after about an hour, the vehicle was righted, and DRIVEN with help, back up the mountain – much to the happiness of the crowd I might add.

If this had happened in Australia – the people may have managed to get out – but the vehicle would have stayed there until a tow truck had been called!
Yes, in India – everyone stops to help. I guess in Australia we are more inclined to lay 'blame' somewhere!

Must rest – as my headache is returning.
And Swami says – Drink MORE water!

08.07.06.

Well – from near hell to near heaven – actually it is Heaven!

Up early, terrible conditions for sleeping – still with a slight headache and nausea, also tingling of the fingers. More burst blood vessels – especially on my ankles and legs – extremities. The road – well the usual – nothing else to add!

Then about 1.00 p.m. in the distance, we all saw Mt. Kailash – the peaks covered in snow! Our vehicle circumnavigated the Tibetan Prayer Flags at the top of the hill; overlooking Lake Manasarovar, with Mt. Kailash as a mighty back drop!
We had finally arrived in God's Land!
Om Namaha Shivaya
Namaha Shivaya
Om Shiva Om.

The Energy of our vantage point about 68-72%.
From the angle we were standing it looked as though the right
hand side of Mt. Kailash, was a snow covered Pyramid.
Oh what great and wondrous beauty to behold!
Any feelings of nausea or sickness disappeared, as all bowed in
reverence to 'THE MIGHTY SHIVA' – Mt.Kailash.

The blue of Lake Manasarovar also a sight to behold –
Om Namaha Shivaya.

As we looked across 'The Lake' the rain began to fall on Kashmir,
however for us – the sun was shining.
Many photos and videos were taken, not by me – the boys did
all!
As we were about to leave, Maj motioned to look at the sun, and
there was the most glorious Rainbow I had ever seen, completely
'encircling' the Sun – quite a way out.
A God Made Miracle – no doubt about THAT!

Soon back to the vehicles and off again, finally reaching the
edge of Lake Manasarovar an hour later.
It was breathtaking emotion to see the entire group, plus some
drivers and sherpas, all paying homage to Manasarovar and Mt.
Kailash.
Some were kneeling in gratitude – some ran to the water's edge
and plunged in, others prayed, some did Puja; all was a sight of
wonderment to behold.

To go through such agony, and then finally to arrive was BLISS!
Pure Joy for the Heart and FOOD FOR THE SOUL!

Back to organization once again! Tents to be pitched and placed
here and there. Finally the helpers realized I needed a single
tent, so mine was to be erected last.

In the meantime – I could wait no longer, so into the water, fully clothed, I went. It was not freezing as I had expected, but moderate in temperature.

I prayed to Baba – Shiva – and did what I had to do for myself, my loved ones, and the Universe in general.

A couple of women suggested gathering some pebbles from the sand – which I did.

I placed my hand in the water and then pulled a handful of sand, then used my fingers as a sieve – so only the pebbles were left. Pebbles were gathered for this one and that one, and a few litres of water as well.

Finally back to the tent area – my lost tent had been found – a small mountain one. I asked for it to be erected a little way away, as there was no room near the boys. Up it went, remembering to ask for the opening to be facing the Lake Manasarovar.

Sheer beauty and gratitude I felt, as I placed my things inside.

Then joy and sheer bliss! I realised, if I lay at one particular end of the tent – I could see Manasarovar and Mt. Kailash as well!

God – this is truly amazing – all the other tents face inwards, and mine is the only one facing towards the lake and mountain. I felt *so* happy!

Changed into warm clothing – and settled to listen to my tape on the Vedas.

'No Vedas,' Baba just said – 'A Shiva Tape!'

So into the tape recorder it went and stopped. I turned it over, and there was 'Arathi' to Baba. I felt so much love and joy for Him and Humanity. Bliss and Joy – all is bountiful.

Then settled to write – looking at the view as well.

From my tent, I look through the Tibetan Prayer flags to Mt. Kailash.

Feeling wonderful – just found out that one or our male group has an International roaming cell phone. Mine was left in Kathmandu, as I was told there was no reception up here.

He laughed and said that I could *not* use the phone if I offered him payment! Spoke to Claire to relay the message of exactly where I was, as she was home right at that moment.

Very happy, very happy, just as well I did not have *my* phone, as I would have been calling 'The World,' and dissipating the Energy.

Well my dear, so this is the joy you have been searching for!

Yes, this is what joy feels like – the experience of bliss and joy!

You weep with emotion to see My Mountain – Mt. Kailash, and My Home – The Home of Shiva and Parvathi.

Oh to have My Parvathi here with me! I mean yes she can come any time as Goddess, however to have come in Physical as well, would have been a test of enduring love. A love like no other! Oh My Parvathi – My Divine Amma, My heart cries for the pain you are going through at this time.

However Your great Beauty – Divinity and Knowledge of GODDESS SUPREME, will *soon* be released for all to see and experience.

Why have I kept you in darkness until now?

Why indeed?

You may well ask.

Timing was premature – much darkness and evil has been spread, and even though you are Goddess, you have been left unprotected.

Even I – Your Shiva – Who is God to all – have experienced areas of difficulty in the Physical World at this time.

I have become more 'aged' – and it is time for my devotees to look within – from the Form to the Formless.

During this period of transition, many will be looking for another Guru, God, or Goddess to worship.

In this period of transition you *will* retain ALL of your 'former' Glory – of this you may be assured!

The 12 Jyotirlinga Work has been completed, and the Energy of The Mother released in all her glory, for all The World to see.

Finally the tying-up of the Energy at Mt.Kailash, and the ruination of Man will be nullified by The Mother.

All will once again bathe in 'The Bliss' of The Mother.

Truth NOW lies in the Bosom of The Mother, for all The World to Experience.

Om Sai Ram.

As The Shiva Energy is unblocked and released – The Energy of The Mother will flow forth – as the welling up of Love blossoms for Mankind.

The 'Welling up' of Love I say, as only LOVE will ultimately SAVE Humanity.

There is no greater LOVE for Man to experience THAN THE LOVE OF SELF – THE GODSELF!

Remember to all –

You and I are ONE

You are God

You are that You are

or

I AM THAT I AM.

Let no one deter you from Your Path.

Lay down your arms and open them for and to – Your Fellow Man.

Truth is ONE
Love is ONE
Seva / Service is most IMPORTANT.

With Truth and Love in your Heart – you must do Seva / Service to help your fellow Man.
Are not ALL Men and Women a brother or sister of God?
I think so.

Now my dear, you enquire about the 'circular' Rainbow?
Rarely do I manifest a Rainbow such as this.
The normal Rainbow you see generally is an accompaniment to rain or threatening rain.
However this one was completely 'circular' in shape, around the Sun, and not near either!
So the great beauty of The Rainbow circumnavigating the Sun, with the view of Manasarovar and Mt. Kailash.

This my dear is a special blessing – rarely seen on Earth at this time.
It signifies COMPLETION of God's Journey – MOKSHA – ENLIGHTENMENT – however only to those who saw it, or were guided to see it.

All who experienced 'this' particular Rainbow, will have this future Human Life – one of bliss and enjoyment, coupled with abundance and contentment. All who thought to ask for a Divine Blessing today – will receive all they ever wish, hope or dream for.

You spend a lot of time my dear praying for others – so you forget yourself. Even this morning you shed a few quiet tears for yourself.

You ask Baba – why cannot you be with me?
Do I have to endure this physical torture for much longer?
Then I show you what will eventuate after you complete
Mt. Kailash, and the tying-up of the Energy for Mankind.

Your job – specific work – has not been easy.
You came to me later than expected, and your health has
not been a priority for you! This I have warned you about
time and time again.
However, because of your tenacity and determination to
complete The Shiva Work for Humanity, you will soon be
much blessed. Your work will finish after your book is
published, and then you may rest or travel, and also see
and enjoy the surprises I have in store for you.

Yes, I gave you a *momentary* Vision, just to ease your pain
of this morning – during your little weep for yourself and
your life. A hard life you have experienced, so bliss and
joy are soon to be yours.

Yes, your trip with this Group was all planned.
The ISOLATION the most important aspect of your life
at this time.
To stand ALONE is powerful, but to feel LONELY is a
sad and sorry state to experience.
You have managed to overcome the most ADVERSE of
circumstances and isolation – to commit yourself to THIS
PARTICULAR TRIP!
I am much pleased with you – much pleased.
And as you know when Baba is pleased – only Blessings
occur.
It is your time NOW!

Om Namaha Shivaya.

Two of the female group members just stopped by to say hello –
enquiring about how often I come to India, and 'who' do I see?
'Sai Baba,' I replied.
'Have you seen the Amma from Kerala – the hugging Amma?'
'Yes, once' I replied.
'How do they compare – which is better?'
'There is no comparison, as she is a Divine Mother.'
I knew they thought she was a Divine Mother, and Baba was a
Guru!
How do you say – one is Mother, and the other is ALL!

Yes my dear, Truth soon will reign supreme.
Soon ALL will see the magnificence of Baba's Leela!
Life is only a Divine Leela after all – soon to be
'announced' for all the World to see and share – in the
beauty of Baba's Bounty and Grace.

Om Namaha Shivaya
Om Om Om.
Om Shanti Om.

Oh my goodness, I have just realised I will be able to see the
setting sun as well.
Blessed, blessed I feel!

09.07.06.

Mid morning Tibet time – all packing up to leave.
Some Shiva Devotees still bathing in Lake Manasarovar – all
chatting and excited about life – their Spiritual life. A great and
wondrous adventure taking place – no question about that!

So what did last night bring?
First of all I had a short rest, with my head pointing towards
Mt.Kailash.

It was glorious!

Shiva was sitting there – looking like we see in the photos!

He then placed his right foot on my head – Crown Chakra, and left foot on my shoulder.

Then he asked me to deeply breathe in The Shiva Energy.

He thumped his Trident to the ground, and as he did, I breathed in the glorious Shiva Energy to every cell of my physicality, but in a uniformed manner – from the top of my head to the soles of my feet, then generally throughout my body – for nine breaths.

All cells turned to 'Om' – All a Golden Om!

During this time I did my own prayer – Puja.

Finally Shiva asked me to have my feet face Mt. Kailash.

I asked a couple of times!

Yes, feet towards Mt. Kailash, as the respect I have for 'your' Journey!

So I turned around in bed.

He touched the soles of my feet and the Energy – Prana – went surging through my body.

Then he came really close to me – it appeared he stretched from Mt. Kailash to Manasarovar – it was amazing.

He then said 'Look at Me,' and came right up to MY face.

It was as if He was holding a mirror, and all I could see was HIS REFLECTION!

'I am You,' I said.

Yes, a job well done – The completion of your Work for Mankind will culminate at Mt. Kailash.

'How will I manage the three day climb?' I asked.

Nandi will be your Pony.'

The Form of Shirdi will be your Pony's helper.'

The Form of Baba will walk with you as your helper.'

My Trident will be your walking stick.
All will be well.
You must listen to me talking – not the speech of others,
who 'think' they know.

Om Namaha Shivaya.

All will be well.
Yes, I hear you – You want to go home two days earlier in
the Helicopter, as there are still two days of strenuous
driving, and then six kilometres of walking.
NO – THIS IS NOT FOR YOU AT THIS TIME!
Do you wait in Kathmandu for the others?
No, you come home to me in Puttaparthi earlier, if your
plans change.

Om Shanti Om.

Only three Darshans, then home to Australia for writing
and rest.
All will be well.
Your body requires rest, and you have accomplished much
my beauty.
Please complete Nancye's book.
Please send me extra copies of Book 3 for some of my
students, to give out when I deem fit for them to receive.
Please have your new book completed by the 17th
September.
Just 3000 copies – that is all.

Yes, yes, I am the black Crow that flew over just this
moment.
Crow Medicine – yes, you have vast amounts of that
Energy as well.
Have a hot drink now.
Baba – Shiva – Lord of The Universe.

THE PARIKRAMA – DAY 1

THE PARIKRAMA – DAY 1.

Interesting to observe we began our journey with sixty travellers plus staff and helpers, and now due to the impossible climbing conditions and extreme physical endurance required, we are twenty in number including staff and helpers.

Up early after a restless night in the tent, and on the way to Mt. Kailash. Apparently we drive the first ten kilometres or so, then walk for the remainder of the day – about 12 kilometres.
It is on the second day we require a Pony or Horse for some of the way, as the path is very steep.

The most glorious walk. For a short while I walked on my own, and then met up with an interesting couple from The States. Cam calls her husband Rama – 'The Kodak Man,' and he surely is! So it was not only an interesting walk, but a very informative one as well.

A much travelled Soul – with boundless energy and extremely interesting knowledge, just happened to float by into my life.

So it was a good mix – the girls walking in front, and then resting on a rock, waiting for Mr. Kodak to arrive, with sherpa in tow.

Where did we stay the first night?
In tents of course!
The organizers thought to place two Indian women with me – all well. Not quite sure where the husbands were!
Eventually I went to partake of some chatter and fun with my walking partner – returning some time later to an empty tent.
Oh yes, my things were all there, but my visitors had deserted me yet once again.
It's been interesting being a single Western Woman.
Oh yes, all smile and say hello – but there definitely is a difference between saying hello, and wanting to share a tent with a Foreigner.

So Swami, You teach us – ALL IS ONE – However is it –
ALL IS ONE – Only if you are Indian?
I must talk seriously to you about this sometime in the future!

Another restless night – the Energy is really high and movable here on the first day of 'The Parikrama,' or the walk around the base of Mt. Kailash!
Must try to sleep – but know already it will be difficult.

The scenery today was magnificent – great beauty to behold.
The climb was not just a stroll! It was a *steep* climb, through areas of rugged terrain, interspersed with green valleys with unusual and interesting shaped rocks!
Being with friends added a new joy and meaning to the walk – a little discussion here and there – 'Food for The Soul'.

THE PARIKRAMA – DAY 2
THE DOLMA PASS

THE PARIKRAMA – DAY 2.

THE ASCENT TO THE DOLMA PASS:

Up early – the hardest day of physical exhaustion looming, and yet excitement mounting!
'The Highway to Heaven' is fast approaching.
However can the remaining few of us, only twenty or so, including the staff and sherpas, actually manage the climb to 'The Dolma Pass' or Dolma–la Pass, nearly 5400 metres or 14,500 feet above sea level?

Previously, the organizers of the trip had suggested we could all hire a horse or pony to help with our travels. Of course I had agreed, so did not understand when they asked – 'Did I want a horse?' Then proceeded to explain – there were no horses / ponies on the first day, then on the second day, some areas were *too* difficult for even a horse, so walking would be a necessity – or freeze to death!

Looking valiantly for my Horseman – he was nowhere to be seen, so decided to begin the walk to where they would be waiting, a little further up the mountain, to an area that looked like a 'landing zone.'

Finally connected with him, and to my absolute horror, a Priest or Llama from our group was trying to persuade the Horseman to give him *my* horse. He suggested I ride the packhorse!

All a bit of a drama – however I stood firm, as I knew *that* particular horse was the only means of transport at *that* time, to help me reach the top of The Pass.

It was there at the top of The Pass I was to finally TIE IN ALL THE ENERGIES OF THE 12 JYOTIR LINGAMS!

I must admit to being a bit disappointed by his actions. He would not have dared do *this* to a Man, and he claimed to be a Swami, a Llama, a Holy Man!

I really could write two books here – one regarding only the Spiritual Energies of the work, and the other about the various personalities and their idiosyncrasies.

However one is more fun, and I will do as Swami says –
'Tell the truth, so long as no-one is hurt!'
'If the Ego is hurt – fine – but *not* the Heart'!

Yesterday my Horseman informed me that he did not like Westerners – especially women. Also that I am too fat, have bad knees, and cannot breathe properly! What a start to the day! He would *not* stop to allow me to walk, drink water, or even put on a raincoat – UNLESS I became very strong and aggressive, or found one of the sherpas, who would *force* him to stop!

Food – you enquire? You must be joking!

Then I remembered the three Mars bars in my pocket, given to me by my new friends, at the beginning of the three-day Parikrama.

That was all I could eat! I gave thanks to the 'Mars' Company so many times, I cannot tell you!

The nausea was overwhelming at times – and when I did feel a need to eat – the Mars bars had frozen in my pocket.

Because of the high altitude, and extremes in physical exercise and endurance, plus the freezing cold – the thought of food made me physically sick as well. Even the zips on my pockets were all frozen.

My body so exhausted and sore – every limb ached, not to mention my back – it felt as though it had broken.

In the evening I was so nauseated from the altitude – again no food!

Somewhere I remember having porridge – one day – sometime – somewhere – that was all!

Climbing The Dolma Pass on horseback first, then by foot, with the help of a sherpa's walking stick!

The terrain so steep and the rocks so huge to climb over!

The Tibetan Prayer Flags blowing in the wind – just a gentle rain at times – snow here and there – but the wind – it was *so* cold!

My fingers were numb, back aching, hip joints ready to explode, knees weak and trembling.

Many times during the ride and walk I prayed to Shiva to 'take me now,' or to help in some way! Then all of a sudden, it was as though a huge set of Electric Currents, looking like a 'knuckle buster' from the slums of New York, were attached to my Spine – THE UNIVERSAL CODE OF CONDUCT, and the Energy would surge forth once again. I recall this happened about three times.

At one point it was so cold, I had given up trying to breathe through my nose to warm the air.

Shiva said – 'Don't worry, I have you in a state of advanced hyperplasia now – just breathe through your nose when you *feel* it is about nine breaths.'

So I tried omitting eight breaths, which I did for maybe five times, then I couldn't breathe at all.

Then Shiva said 'Don't worry – I will look after you'!

There was no way 'I' managed to climb THAT Mountain Pass, without God's help!
NO WAY ON EARTH!

THE DOLMA PASS:

Upon reaching the top of The Pass, and TYING UP ALL THE ENERGIES OF THE 12 JYOTIR LINGAMS, I felt the work had been completed, to some degree I guess.

Then I was told to 'recalibrate' the Energies of the 12 Lingams again – which I did.

It was as though the whole 12 Energies were 'looped' around Mt. Kailash, quite tightly.

I remember breathing a sigh of relief – thinking the work was now complete, also remembering to send prayers and thanks to all, and instigated some special requests.

I must confess – when you experience such agony – to experience even one moment of bliss, is a wonder and joy in itself!

At the top of The Dolma Pass the wind was blowing so strongly, the sky brilliant blue – then turning to darker grey a long way down the mountain. It was a truly wondrous sight to behold!

I heard later that the maximum time one can spend at the top of the Pass is four minutes. Now that would have been good to know before hand!

Some of the boys and sherpas took photos – which I am yet to see!

THE DESCENT FROM THE DOLMA PASS

Unfortunately my horse was not available again, so I paired up with Cam, whilst Rama walked behind enjoying the scenery, taking videos and photos.

Down, down we descended – so steep at times I had to use my hands to grasp the rocks and boulders.
Fortunately my 'trusty' walking stick never far from my right hand. There was no way I could have descended and negotiated 'The Pass' without a stick! Sometimes the rocks and path so steep – three feet or more, from one level to another.
Running steams, beginning to melt, here and there to cross.

The Poles!
The bridges are only made of poles strung together.
The Tibetans tie two or three poles together with wire, loosely running a parallel. The minute your foot touches one – they ALL move! Help!
Once or twice I had to negotiate a stream of rapids by myself! The choice was to stay where I was and freeze to death waiting for someone to help, or try by myself. So after many prayers yet again, I bravely crossed, trying not to look at the rapids below. Once again, I guess if I had been back home I would have waited for help.

Down, down, and yet further down we descended, until I saw a 'Glacier' type of thing. At first I couldn't believe my eyes – as the snow was already melting around the edges, and some parts of the middle as well.
HELP!
Fortunately Cam came to the rescue with her Ski Pole – and gently holding my hand, we ever so carefully tiptoed across. After a few testing moments we were safely on the other side.

And so the day went, until eventually I found my Horseman again. Once again the usual difficulties mounting the horse. Having limited riding experience, it didn't take a Rhodes Scholar to figure out it would have been so much easier to mount the horse, if it had been brought alongside a rock! Let me tell you – and there were plenty of those everywhere!

No – he insisted – so it was always a standing mount, as his horse was very temperamental – and yes, I can vouch for that as well! He had to tie the hind legs together before I mounted each time.

Somewhere on that second day whilst climbing up The Dolma Pass, I remember Rama showing us the Shiva / Shakti or Shiva and Parvathi Rocks! Knowledge – knowledge – what an abundance of knowledge he had! It was rare to meet a couple that had seen 10 of the 12 Jyotir Lingams.

One thing about the trip – the variety of people, or let us say the personality idiosyncrasies of some of the group, I have found most interesting.
It has not been easy being the only Westerner, with sixty Indian Nationals and twenty Nepalese.
God surely singled me out as 'different' this time!
In fact, even visiting the 12 Jyotir Lingams in all those different States in India, apart from hearing there were a couple of tourists in Varanasi – I never saw one Western face.

The latter part of Day 2 was a continual blur – suffering from cold, praying to God to save me – and promising I would never leave Australia again.
All I did was either pray to be saved, or pray to die NOW!
'Please take me soon if this is the amount of pain I have to endure,' I kept repeating to myself.

Then Shiva's Hand would move to my spine, and again he would say – 'NOW you are plugged in to The Universal Code of Conduct.'

'You are now using Hydro-trophic Breath Work – just rest and let ME do the work'!

So I would close my eyes – I could hardly see anyway, and drift into a state of altered reality for a while. Mind you, while still being acutely aware of the agony going on in the saddle.

After a short while I dismounted, and had no feeling in my legs momentarily, however prayed, and then the Energy came surging through again!

So after a few testing moments – off I bounded – not really that short of breath either!

Eventually after another bout of riding, I arrived at the camp, one of the first!

Many tents were being erected, and I remembered thinking – 'I need to rest NOW,' as I was shivering, and the nausea was returning.

'This tent will do!' I said in a firm voice – knowing they preferred to settle the couples or groups first. So I stood beside the tent vomiting – and up it went! As per usual no-one wanted to join me – a blessing most of the time I must admit, however a little frightening when you are really sick and may require some help.

Not to worry – Penta and also his cousin Cammie, my young Sherpa friends, were soon there to see if I was alright, – asking me what I would like for dinner or to drink!

They even helped me off with my heavy clothes, as by then I could not bend at all!

Two young Sherpa boys that certainly made a huge difference to my whole trip – thank you God!

Probably the most uncomfortable night thus far – the extremes of exhaustion from the physical exertion and riding, plus the altitude, nearly 5400 metres.

A tent without a comfortable base is not the way to go – and on a slope as well!

Also the Energy work did not help induce a peaceful night's sleep either!

THE PARIKRAMA – DAY 3

THE PARIKRAMA – DAY 3.

Up early, apparently it is only a short walk today!
A ride on the horse, more walking, and then the vehicle will be
waiting on the other side of the mountain, to take us back to the
safety of Manasarovar.

No Horseman in sight – so yet again began the trek by myself.
After about two hours I began to 'fade' rapidly. After crossing
one of the 'fort' bridges again, I looked back many kilometres –
and still no horse!
It was then I prayed to God – as I knew I just could not make
the last ten kilometres on my own!
Then in the distance I saw the elusive horseman, with his two
horses, just nonchalantly walking along. In fact most of the way
I had walked, I could have ridden! So I perched on a rock and
patiently waited.
Standing mount again!
Oh yes, the saddle was only covered by a single Tibetan rug –
not 'padded' like the other saddles.

We had honestly only ridden for less than an hour, when he said, 'NO MORE HORSE – HORSE FINISHES HERE!'
'Excuse me,' I exclaimed.
Yes – all the area I had just walked, was horse turf – now it was too steep and too dangerous!

You could have knocked me over with a feather!
I dismounted – he demanded money – I gave him his fare. He was pleasantly relieved I gave freely, as I could see he was expecting a disagreement or argument. He then offered to carry my backpack to the end of the track on his horse, so I waved yet more money in front of him.
Love of money is the Root of all Evil – but sometimes a necessary evil!

I fixed my gaze firmly skywards.
How on Earth was I ever going to climb up that steep mountain, before the more gentle slopes began?
Yet once again I prayed, and a huge 'wave' of Energy coursed through my veins. My breathing almost non-existent – so more hydro-trophic breath work!

Please send someone to help me I prayed in absolute earnest!
Soon a young Tibetan boy appeared. He was a sherpa from our group – one I had *never* seen before!
'Here, take my arm and let me carry your water – I will help you the last part of the way'.

On and on we walked – the distance never ending. I just kept looking at the valley below – the rivers, the terrain – the thought of the never-ending path almost too much to bear.
At times the path of loose red gravel was only 10-12 inches wide, and it was a long drop to the river below.

Oh how pleased I was to have a comforting arm to hold on to for support. The young man was extremely interested in all areas of life, and asked where I had been, what my views were on certain aspects of life. General and yet profound questions being asked, and answered!

Finally, after many hours of walking, when I knew my tired old body could not take anymore, we rounded a cliff and there a short distance away was the Number Plate – AA9210!
I thought it was a mirage!
I looked again – yes – it was the trusty old Toyota Land Cruiser!
Neemah our driver had managed to park nearest to the walking track, at the completion of the walk!

I was so overjoyed; I dragged myself up to his window, and put my arms around his neck, and sobbed and sobbed!
I just could not talk!
He patted my back – poor fellow – probably never had a Western Woman hugging him in tears. He helped me into the car to keep warm. Oh to be warm and at home in the car again!

Let me tell you – I have driven and owned some fairly fancy cars in my day – but THIS old, dilapidated, 12 year old Land Cruiser, was the best car I had *ever* seen!

As for my Tibetan friend – I NEVER SAW HIM AGAIN!
So WHO was He Really?

LAKE MANASAROVAR:

After the usual IST (Indian Stretchable Time) of wait and see, our small group drove down the mountain to once again camp at Lake Manasarovar – at the water's edge.
Lots of jubilation and general chitchat. Most of the pain and discomfort – lost in a brief moment of bliss and joy!
A tiny dispute over where to pitch the tents. Some wanted a more sheltered position further back, but the majority wanted to be near the Lake. Needless to say – The Lake won!

By this time, my general level of exhaustion had increased dramatically, and all I wanted was a mattress to rest my weary body on!

Soon we were all bedded down for the night.

Already the wind was blowing quite ferociously – my tent cover flapping valiantly in the breeze – so still more adjustments. Eventually settled for the night – and what a night it was!

The wind blew and blew – the tent was freezing, and my body so cold I could not move my legs at all!

'Help' I thought – I will die here, so crawled out of the tent to seek a bit of help, as the water was flowing under the sleeping mattress.

Surprise, surprise, only a few tents were still there – the rest of the group, plus our tour group leaders, had all moved to a more sheltered position, quite a distance away.

What would have happened in an emergency?

Then pondered on a few platitudes of thought – not so pleasant either!

Up early – that part was not too difficult, as I could not sleep anyway. Prayed a lot for help – especially for my legs, chest and lungs.

Encountered a minor problem when I tried to pull my tracksuit pants over my thermals, and could not move my right leg at all – help! Then along came one of the young Sherpas, and helped me with the tracksuit, then obligingly helped me with my shoes as well. Slowly he pulled me to my feet.

All is as it should be – I guess!

It was mentioned later on that couple of pilgrims had died during the trek due to extreme physical exhaustion and oxygen deprivation.

MANASAROVAR – KATHMANDU:

It was a little later the boys suggested we drive straight though to Saga – 400 kilometres, as all were experiencing *varying* degrees of exhaustion and debilitation!
It sounded like a good idea to me at the time!

16.07.06.

Up early – 4.30 a.m. and ready to leave by 5.00 a.m.
Another reasonable night thank goodness.
Today we are driving straight through to Kathmandu.
A few more hours in Tibet, the Chinese Border, the Nepalese Border, and finally into Nepal.

6.45 p.m.

Well – all did not go as smoothly as anticipated, or maybe I should say everything went as per usual – would be a more apt description.

The landscape was glorious, with waterfalls, greenery, and great mountainous beauty. How can the terrain change from so bleak to so lush, in such a short span of time?

THE CHINESE – TIBET BORDER:

The traffic banked up for many kilometres – what a depressing experience. Eventually we all walked on foot to the 'actual' checkpoint.
Encountered another few hours standing – waiting – another totally debilitating experience. Finally up to the security desk, as I was first in our group – not that I was special – just 'A' for Australia, then through the checkpoint.

Here I must pass comment on the 'Laser Gun.'

On the way through the checkpoint, a laser gun had been held up to my third eye, and the number 33.1 branded on my forehead area – easily readable on the dial. The experience happened so quickly I did not even have time to protect myself! Then on the way out of Tibet, the same reading again! Big Brother was and is everywhere!

Eventually we located our land cruiser and fell into the front seat, for our final six-kilometre drive down to the Nepalese Border.

Many forms to be filled out yet once again, and much to my grief, I realised I did not have another passport photo. The previous visa – two weeks back, had been only validated for two days, not two weeks!

After a gruelling few moments I decided to find the most *important* looking person there. He was very understanding and amiable – 'Just tell the men to see me!'

Another long wait, then eventually he emerged from his office, smiled, and beckoned me over. I guess he knew I would still be there at midnight otherwise, as hundreds of people were waiting!

A hug and goodbye to my friend and driver Neemah, a generous tip goes without saying! Finally a short walk over The Friendship Bridge into Nepal, and on to lunch.

One of my friendly sherpas carrying my backpack and water, so not too stressful!

Lunch – the restaurant absolutely brimming with people, with no room downstairs, so I decided to sit on the balcony in a corner – where the stairs turn upwards.

Lunch very tasty and very spicy – and once again contemplated the 'aloneness' factor.

The Indians definitely treat Westerners differently; there is no question about that. There would have been room at a table if all had squeezed up together, but it was not meant to be for me on this trip. At home we would have pulled a chair out of thin air, to help accommodate a newcomer!

Another huge learning.

They form their own special groups, and never change from that particular environment.

At the time I saw it as a rather 'limited' vision to and for others! Have I unintentionally maybe done this to others myself?

It has been a hard and difficult experience travelling with sixty-two Indians. The Sherpas and drivers seem to be friendly, but the Group seemed to come for *their* Pilgrimage, and kept to themselves. To be honest – that is what a 'true' Pilgrimage should be all about!

Being in the presence of God, or listening to the voice of God!

So who had the problem – maybe it was me!

Maybe I had better look at 'Expectations' again!

I know when I am with Sunita I never encounter problems of separation. Is it because she is with her friends? Is it because I am with her? Or are we referring to grace and manners?

Darkness has fallen and we are still in a traffic jam – so must stop writing now. There has been an accident between a newly married couple on a motorcycle, and a bus. The couple were killed! Feeling blessed to be alive, as we passed the couple lying on the side of the road. Oh dear what Karma!

17.07.06.

KATHMANDU – NEPAL:

Here we all are in The Royal Singh Hotel. It's a little more upmarket than the other hotel, and you would have to ask – why the move? A few minor problems here and there – by now I have *almost* mastered the emotions of NO expectations, and patience.

We arrived in Kathmandu about 8.00 p.m. I think – all a bit of haze. Finally after finding my 'stored' luggage – we caught a taxi and proceeded back to the new hotel.
Great room – even a bath, however a quick shower and into bed.

On a scale of 1-10, my body pain is about a 6, so almost bearable again. A little concerned over my medical cover – insurance from home, so I had better look into that quickly. To find out I am uninsured may be a problem later on, if medical cover is required.

Thinking about Manasarovar – yet again.
I remember lying in the cold, damp tent praying, then all of a sudden Shiva was there – and even now I remember the exact words He uttered –

You have 'linked up' all of the Energy of the 12 Jyotirlingas, so you may cut or release the Energy Ties all individually NOW!

This must be a mistake – the wrong information!
To have worked so hard, or let us say – to have DRAGGED the Energies of the 12 Jyotir Lingams all the way up The Dolma Pass to 5400 metres, and linked / looped the 12 Jyotir Lingam Energies individually around Mt. Kailash, only to be told – to RELEASE them all individually or as a collective!
Shiva must be joking!
I felt devastated, and as though I had done everything I had been told, as best I could, considering my human frailties – and then told to cut and release ALL the ties back to their 'own' destinations!
Because of my reluctance and hesitancy Shiva was there –

191

It is easy – look!

As he walked around Mt. Kailash, and slipped the individual loops off the mountain, and then cut the energetic cords, connecting all!

Snip, snip, snip – see!

The Energy Cords recoiled immediately, and literally flew straight back to their 'own' specific destinations in India.
It was as though the Energy of each individual Lingam *then* intensified!

NOW ALL WILL BE TRUTH – SATHYA – ALL WILL BE WELL.

Om Namaha Shivaya.

This morning as I was writing, Shiva said that I had completed really difficult work.

To reattach the 12 Energetic Cords will be easy for you now. So please attach them NOW!

So I picked up the Energetic Loops of the individual 12 Lingams, and collectively placed them all around Mt. Kailash. Then I was told to 'tighten' them up yet once again. So I did – no problem!

Leave them around me for 12-18 hours – I will decide then.

Om Namaha Shivaya.

This morning whilst clearing out the duffle bag from the trip, I found a golden coloured Conch. It was not there before, so more Shiva moments of encouragement.

Baba has said to not waste my time in Puttaparthi, at this stage of my journey. I am to go home and complete the book as soon as possible. I guess that is what I will do.

He also said not to look at 'His Physicality' in Puttaparthi anymore, and just to see Lord Shiva everywhere.

Also I am to offer my services to Amma – Parvathi – Rajarajeshwari – in Mysore.

So I guess my life is about to change rapidly, and that is fine as well. To be honest, I feel as though I have earned a place in Heaven.

Without a doubt, this has been the most exhausting – mentally, emotionally, physically and Spiritually debilitating Journey – of my entire life!

Life has been a bit of a challenge here and there, no question about that. But right now, as the tears run down my cheeks, I would have to say – I am not sure if I have been to Heaven on Earth or Hell on Earth. I have just realised they are two sides of the ONE coin anyway!

Still experiencing a little of – Why me?

Why not – someone else?

Why was I not born normal?

And then I know I really have had no choice, and if I was asked to do it all again – My Irene Self says no – however my God Self says – NO CHOICE!

ONCE is all it takes for any Human Being or Animal – Just ONCE!

I am still experiencing chest / coughing problems, so had better look at that as well. Apparently there is a condition developed during the rigorous breathing on the mountain pass called 'The Kailash Cough!' It is not really a cough as such – more like a deep bark!

At least it is great being back in civilisation, even though my Spirits are a bit low, and my body still aching.

We are all leaving about 1.30 p.m. for the airport – another long day ahead. Kathmandu – Delhi – then another change of planes to Bangalore.
There do not seem to be any reserves left at this stage, and of course I can't carry anything at all!
Maybe I should ring Sunita and ask for help?

KATHMANDU – DELHI:

The flight from Kathmandu to Delhi was fine – King Fisher Air. Waved goodbye to the boys – the two young sherpas who had helped me so *very* much during the trip. Both aged about 30 years. How would I have managed without them? Well – we know the answer to that question! Most probably I would have been another statistic by now!

After sixteen days together, only in the last moments did some of the group speak with me. They began enquiring as to my flight details. You could have knocked me over with a feather – English! I guess the 'Cultural' differences are what surprised me the most at times!

All boarded the bus – mainly the male section of the group.
I was totally unable to lift my luggage up the stairs of the bus. Unless you specifically ASK for help – no one offers. Finally upon boarding the bus I asked a gentleman for assistance. Instead of helping – he called to two elderly women to lift the bags. I nearly died of embarrassment – they were my age! Let me tell you, I was not too popular after that experience!

Another flight home to Bangalore, where I was met by my driver Vinod – what a gentle Soul. He had found my Baba and Christ pendant. The minute I slipped it on – all felt wonderful momentarily.

RETURN TO PUTTAPARTHI:

A good night's rest, then off to the Publishers – Book Work –
then eventually to Puttaparthi to see Baba for three Darshans!

**Do not come to see me unless you see my Form as only
LORD SHIVA!**
**You are not to look at the poor health and physicality of an
80 year old elder.**
THIS IS NOT WHO I AM!

Stayed with Rika and Rama.
Feeling a little better, so sorted through some clothes – saris, and
generally rested for one day.
The feeling to see Baba was just *not* there! I knew that if I saw
him in the 'physical' I would *still* see him as Baba, so no Darshan
for me!
It felt fine not going inside the Ashram as well.

Apparently Baba has had a few 'not so good' days. His health is
once again in a questionable state. He appears extremely weak,
and at times a little disorientated.

I remember in Whitefield, when Baba was retelling the story of
'Sita and Rama' – the tears would well up in His eyes, and He
had a tremor in his voice.

So Lord Shiva is REIGNING SUPREME at this moment in time!
I remember from the Jyotir Lingam Work – the knowing that
after the Shiva work completed at each Lingam, then with 'this
completion' came a standing back!
Finally with firm resolve – allowing the Energies of The Mother,
Divine Mother, to blossom forth in all HER Glory!

Om Sai Ram.

Yes, and Mother Earth – The Goddess Energy – All Female Forms of The Divine – will once again RULE The Earth. After a period of catastrophe and ADJUSTMENT all will eventually flow with The Divine River of Light and Love.

Cleansing, cleansing, will alter the very fibre of every Human Being, during this period of adjustment – until Mother Earth has released all her Energy yet once again. Then and only then one can truly say –

DIVINITY IS AND WILL NOW ALWAYS BE – CONTAINED IN THE WOMB OF THE MOTHER!

The Divine Feminine is about to burst forth in all her GLORY, and change The Dharmic Path of EXISTENCE forever.

Om Sai Ram.

Go home sweet prince and write this story. Many are waiting to see and read the written word. Please be vigilant and do not waste time, energy or money!

So you crawled into Puttaparthi and did not see me. Why?
Because you could *not* see me ONLY AS SHIVA.

When you look at me in my Physical Form – what do you ALL see?
You see the persona of an 80 year old elder.
You all do *not* see TRUTH – The Truth of 'Who I Am!'
So, Who Am I Really?
Well, the answer to this you must know by now, however still the 'Physical' Form baffles most.
The reality of the illusion – is a further illusion still.

You all come; you observe, you instil in your hearts and minds A COMPLETE PICTURE OF WHO YOU THINK I AM.
All an illusion of your overactive Monkey Mind, I might dare to say.

You came – you listened to My Words – You left to go home.
All was perfect timing – perfect!
So home you went and into bed for two weeks – with another pelvic displacement.

The Shiva Work has been far more extensive than ever you could have imagined my dear. Now nearly three weeks later your lower back and pelvis are only NOW beginning to slowly move towards a 'healing' solution.

Be gentle on yourself – Each time you alter the Energy of one Lingam – the others slightly 'shift' as well.
The 12 Jyotirlingas are still 'recovering,' and require further Energetic Compensatory Work – to bring them all into alignment with GLOBAL HARMONY, and then total Global Harmonics.

Again you ask?
Yes, thousands of years have past since the event of Global Harmonics.

SOON – ALL WILL COME TO PASS.

Om Sai Ram.

THE
ATHI RUDRA
MAHA YAGNA

YAGNA

'The inner meaning of Yagna is 'renunciation, sacrifice or giving up'.
For whom?
For The Divine Lord!

The heart that you gave me, I am offering it in return, is the spirit of renunciation. The heart He has given, the feelings He evokes, the wealth He has conferred, the fame He has awarded – these have to be gladly offered back'.
SSS Vol XI Chapter 49 Page 282.

'The external Yagna is only a reflection of the internal Yagna. Through the performance of the Yagna by rituals, religious practices and righteous deeds, the inner self is purified'.

'Man should offer to the Divine his pure unselfish heart, and such noble qualities such as Sathya – Truth, Dharma – Righteousness, Santhi – Peace, Prema - Love, Compassion and Love of all beings'.
SS.Oct.2003.

THE ATHI RUDRA MAHA YAGNA

This Yagna is conducted for the welfare of the world. There is a very important aspect of this Yagna. The Athi Rudra Maha Yagna protects and fosters the divine nature in the human beings, while rejecting and diminishing the demonic qualities. Thus, it works for the welfare of humanity.

Time and again in the history of human evolution, there come watersheds that redirect humanity towards the ultimate goal. Akin to the loving hands of the mother that support and steady the faltering steps of her toddler, God grants us a glimpse of His Grandeur and what He holds in store for us, with just a small inkling being given in such instances as this.

The Athi Rudra Maha Yagna is the highest form of worship of Lord Shiva. At present the same Athi Rudra is being performed in the presence of Rudra Himself – Sri Sathya Sai Baba. This yagna is for the spiritual progress of humanity as a whole. At the same time it is the duty of each one of us to express our gratitude for our existence, and also to spread the message of love and peace, highlighted by Bhagawan so that His dream of establishing a Nation of Humanity is realized.

The Athi Rudra Maha Yagnam is yet another milestone in the unfolding grand mission of Bhagawan and as significant and far-reaching in its influence as any other; be it the Health, Educare, or Sociocare mission.

THE
ATHI RUDRA
MAHA YAGNA – DAY 1

THE YAGNA – DAY 1: ACTIVATION –
OF LAND MASS SEQUENCES, GRID LINES &
ENERGETIC EQUATIONS.

09.08.06.
9.00p.m

Home in Australia, only to hear Swami was about to conduct an
11-Day Shiva Yagna at Prashanthi Nilayam – The Abode of
Peace – Puttaparthi, Southern India.
Apparently the entire event will take place inside the Kulwant
Hall – with many Priests in attendance.

The correlation between the work that had just been completed,
the energetic 'linking up' of The 12 Jyotir Lingams around Mt.
Kailash, and the clearing of the corrupt and convoluted Shiva
Energy, now seems to be *more* apparent.

**AS THE DIVINE MOTHER – SHAKTI ENERGY
SWEEPS THE EARTH – OH HOW THE DHARMIC
PATTERN OF EXISTENCE WILL CHANGE FOREVER
THE WAYS AND HABITS OF MANKIND IN GENERAL.**

The first day of The Shiva Yagna in India.
Oh how I wish I could have been embroiled in the more 'formal'
energy in India, as opposed to here in Australia.
Whilst driving home this evening I noticed it was a full moon.
The sky was red and glorious.
So what of today dear Heavenly Father?

**The Energy of the land mass has overcompensated for
the changes in the Sea levels for eons.**
This NOW has come to pass.
What has come to pass you ask?
**The changes in the Atmospheric Pressures bring little
relief and help – to a worsening Global situation.**

In other words – today – Day 1 – is all about Mathematics
relating to the Environmental changes within The Universe – all
Universes.
When one land mass experiences Energetic Land Mass Changes,
then a 'Cord' occurs.

A 'Cord' is a numbered mathematical line or linage that is
compounded and re-compounded by a differential of opposites,
until it is basically ready to explode into neutrality.
It compounds and re-compounds time and time again until all
begins to stabilise. This is rare – as all begins to break down and
explode, into another 'Parallel' Universe.

All you have to recognize is that Day 1 of The Shiva Yagna is
THE ACTIVATION OF AND FOR ENVIRONMENTAL
CHANGES.
These changes will ultimately form the basis of harmony in The
Universe – allowing both Global and Universal Harmony to occur.

So first the 'Activation' or great and wondrous Disruption –
followed by the Harmonic Phase – this is only a 24 hour
'intervention' at this early stage.

The 12 Jyotir Lingams are to be 'tightened' energetically by one third this evening, in readiness for Day 2.

By tightening – it is meant the Energetic ties from the individual 12 Lingams will be banded together and looped, and then tightened around Mt. Kailash.

So the 'pivotal' Point of Reference for ALL the Lingam Work during the Yagna time – is Mt. Kailash.

Om Sai Ram.

THE
ATHI RUDRA
MAHA YAGNA – DAY 2

THE YAGNA – DAY 2: ASSIMILATION.

10.08.06.

To assimilate all of our personal, environmental and global differences and negative qualities, into a formidable mass – The Mass of Self Destruction.
This is 'The Mass' pricking our Conscience as Consciousness.
Awareness begins to creep in to every aspect of our being.
The more the *opening* to a higher purpose – the more the *opening* to the Negative aspect of our ultimate Reality.
So Who Are We Really? We all ask time and time again!

We know 'Who' we really are – however what the real underlying problem is – is our inability to ACCEPT 'Who' We Really Are!

As we are given the opportunity to ACCEPT the Negative Aspect of Self – so given the opportunity to 'explore' the Negative Aspect of Self – we feel as though we are continually – MINING THE DARK!

More and more, we mine 'The Dark.'
We ponder, sulk, cry, and try our best to accept our great beauty,
as well as our flaws.
However, the inner beauty of Self fades, as a relentless obsession
with our Negative aspect of Self begins to enfold – and saturate
the very Core of our Existence, or so it appears!

Every fibre of our Being cries –
Is this me?
Is this all that I am?
As we yet once again submerge ourselves in the POWER OF
NOW!

What is The Power of Now?
One is taught – it is to live in the PRESENT!
The Power of Now – Present – Yes, this is truth, however which
Truth?

Is there more than one Truth?
Yes.
There is God's Truth and Your Truth, or God's Truth and Ego
Truth.
The EGO Truth is SURVIVAL!
So who will win?
Your Heart – open and vulnerable, or Your Head – firm and
deliberate?
In this instance 'NOW' is dictated by the Ego, in the form of
escapism – TV etc!

The higher the degree of emergence in the God Self, the nearer
to our goal, or The Goal of Absolution and Enlightenment.
However, it feels as though this ALL comes at a COST!

The nearer to our goal of Freedom – the higher the elevation in
Ego Consciousness to sabotage this Truth?
IS THIS A TRUTH?
IS THIS THE ULTIMATE REALITY?

Will we never be able to make it to The Ultimate Reality, or do we *think* we have found the 'Ultimate' Reality?

Is this Truth?
Or is this Ego Truth?
Remember – many who APPEAR to be the most pious – are not!
APPEARANCE is the greatest MYTH, and the greatest MISCONCEPTION.
Keeping up Appearances – an exhausting experience for and to The Soul of Man.
Is this not what we all try to avoid – and yet ultimately do?
'Appearance' is the DISGUISE OF THE EGO!
Remember, we MIRROR – 'Who' we THINK we really are, as well as KNOW 'Who' we really are!

Wars / Famine / Drought – all basically and fundamentally OBSCURE the Truth of our Reality.
Wars – We look and observe the futility and abhorrence of wars.
Death and Destruction of innocent lives – and ruination of Property and Nations.
The Infrastructure crumbles – ALL Infrastructures crumble!
The Infrastructure of our Essence of Self crumbles!

We observe, if we are not deeply involved in the War. We pass judgement and condemn those *apparent* Powers we believe to be UNDERVALUING the level of Human Existence.
Rarely can we observe war / famine / drought – without passing judgement.
Why do we feel we have the right to Judge?
Because we are still submerged in and with our own IDENTITY – THE EGO OR MORAL CODE OF CONDUCT.

Wars / famine / drought – have always been a part of life, or in the olden days was it not called – SURVIVAL OF THE FITTEST?

Please look through 'The Mirror of Maya' to a place deep within to The God Self. Then ask The God Self – 'Should I Judge?'
Judgement and non-judgement, are two very powerful aspects of THE EGO.
If you feel at any time the need to qualify, quantify, or judge a particular situation – Personal or Global – You are still within the Realms of your Physical Being – The Ego.

Who are You to Judge?
No Judgement should ever take place!
I ALONE AM THE JUDGE OF AND FOR MANKIND – NO OTHER.
Unless you 'judge' from an enlightened perspective – an impossibility in itself – You cannot judge.
I ALONE AM THE JUDGE OF / FOR MANKIND!

So we observe the horror – the atrocities, blatantly being accessed on our newspapers and TV screens.
We observe and *try* not to Judge.
We *try* to remain in a place of NON-JUDGEMENT – pretending to observe and not take sides – as we *still* sit and read and observe the war / famine / droughts.

Can we really sit at such a high level of Consciousness – to be non-judgemental?
Some believe they can – this is their Truth.
Not necessarily THE TRUTH – however THEIR TRUTH.
Why is this so?

Because by seeing, reading or hearing about areas of conflict – wars – poverty – death and destruction, not to mention Environmental SLAUGHTER – we absorb the Energy of 'What it is', we are trying desperately trying to AVOID, at all costs!

As the Negative Energy rises, as in most cases of mass destruction and fear, the energy increases spontaneously, and then we absorb INTRA-CELLULARLY though the Energies, Frequencies and Vibrations (EFV) globally, what others are doing, saying, hearing.
Are we not ALL ONE?
So War in Iraq, Israel, Lebanon, threatens not only the survival of that Nation and their people – but on a cellular level – Our very own survival as well!
THEY experience FEAR – WE experience FEAR.

However, how well can we MASK our Fear – is what we all want to know!
On a cellular level – Fear is being activated in our cells – our DNA feels comfortable surrounded by FEAR – otherwise we would NOT BE HERE AT THIS TIME!

Now you have to ask – So what is the answer to this ponderous question?
The answer is simple – War is the EXCUSE to exacerbate fear within our Essence of Self, and allow us an opportunity to experience the 'bliss' of grace, by rendering us non-judgemental, and in the NOW.

This is only a partial Truth.
We experience ALL in and on many levels – Parallel Universes, Simultaneous lives or Existences.
We are only 'supposedly' Conscious in THIS altered Reality of NOW – The Present, and in this Space.

If wars, death and destruction are occurring in our Universe at THIS time, which they are – then our Energy, Frequency and Vibration (EFV) Rate is altered to accommodate the Global Changes – at THIS time.
Global EFV rise – Personal EFV rise – because ALL IS ONE.

What can we do to help then you ask?
IF ALL IS ONE – and great FEAR is being generated, then
ACKNOWLEDGE THIS FEAR – ACKNOWLEDGE WAR –
DEATH – DESTRUCTION and allow the 'acknowledgement'
to RELEASE from our own cells – from our Molecular Behaviour
Patterning.

Wars give us the 'excuse' needed to work on ourselves.
Do not see yourself as separate from people in War torn areas.
See yourselves as A COLLECTIVE CONSCIOUSNESS.

They experience pain, fear, hunger, remorse – then you 'allow'
yourself to experience the same.
It is in your cells anyway, so why not utilise this great
OPPORTUNTIY TO SET YOURSELF FREE FROM THE
CHAINS THAT BIND YOU!

Absorb the Negative influences and effects of the environment
at present, into the cells of your Being. You are absorbing the
Energy anyway, so why not just accept the EFV are extremely
high at present. They are causing havoc at present – and
ALLOW TRANSFORMATION for and of yourself to take
place.

Transformation can and will occur if you ALLOW it to proceed.
You ALLOW and all flows – You disallow – and all will *not*
flow.
If you *persist* in disallowing Transformation to occur, by not
acknowledging the war and terror within your own make-up or
cells, then you will still remain masked in 'The Ego of Existence'.

This is the greatest opportunity for transformation to occur, during
the heightened times of Global Destruction.
If you feel you have *allowed* your cells to breathe the Negativity
of the Self Destructive Behaviour and Patterning, then you will
be by now experiencing periods and times of bliss.

As you release – more love for yourself and therefore for Humanity – flows forth into your heart.

This LOVE fills the empty crevices, and courses through your veins.

The river of light and love flows freely!

The more you absorb and release the Negative Aspect of Self and Humanity – the more LOVE surrounds the very Core of Your Existence – Your Existence – Other's Existence.

So absorb Global Fear, Death and Destruction, and bathe in the bliss of Human Transformation, as LOVE surges through your veins – as RELEASE takes place.

DEATH → ABSORBTION → TRANSFORMATION → RELEASE → LOVE → HEALING OF THE UNIVERSE.

So it goes.

Allow this time in the History of Mankind, as an opportunity to experience the highest level of growth.

Only by 'allowing' yourself *this* opportunity – will you be able to encapsulate enough LOVE to help healing – Personally and then Globally.

Others are, and have always been a reflection of oneself.

It may not 'appear' to be so at times, however 'Appearances' can be DECEPTIVE!

As we discussed previously – APPEARANCE IS THE MASK OF THE EGO!

Om Sai Ram.

THE
ATHI RUDRA
MAHA YAGNA – DAY 3

THE YAGNA – DAY 3: RETRIBUTION

11.08.06

Yes, it is time for Global Retribution!
This occurs when one deflects and rejects, the Glory of God.
Some call it 'An Eye for an Eye' – or in more simple terms –
PAY BACK!
Yes, it is Global Payback time.

For years Humans have enjoyed the very social, political and
environmental changes – these circumstances that invade and
pervade their lives.
They take – have taken – until the rivers and lakes become
polluted, by individual and global waste and filth.

The business opportunities afforded and accorded – by mining
the land – Our Land – the land left by our Ancestors.
The land they envisaged would be cultivated, provide food and
crops – fodder for the animals. A specific 'need' yet once again
fulfilled and accomplished.

No – we suck the land dry! No preservation is on the minds of those in positions of Power. There is only ONE thought envisaged and visioned – Let us utilise the Environment to fulfil OUR SPECIAL NEEDS, DESIRES AND WANTS!

So it was, and so it still is – in many sections of the Globe.
The good living being harvested by a few – being still outstripped by the megalomania of those in Power.
The Egos of few – RULE the World!

The land suffers, and the environment in general suffers.
The farmers suffer – the shopkeepers suffer – until the end of the line.
Who is waiting at the end of the line?
It is YOU – it is ME – WE all are waiting at the end of the line for fresh produce, a bowl of rice, clean drinking water, a slice of uninfected meat, or disease free chicken.
The normal 'everyday' person suffers – NOT THOSE OF YOU IN POSITIONS OF POWER!

So the Governments make the RULES to 'feather' and further their commitments and strengths to 'other' Governments and Powers.
Yes, at all costs – we require and need to keep happy – OUR ALLIES!

They huddle together like a hoard of Criminals – Plotting, planning, discussing, and then strategising.
Not about how to stop, prevent, minimise or reduce the damage industrialisation and wars are having on the Global Environment and Economy.

No, it is about how we fight our way through this mess to still 'look good' – and yet TAKE something we WANT!

What do 'they' – the Governments in Power really WANT?
Maybe our water, maybe our land?
The more of these precious commodities one has at their disposal,
the more the Countries attain a 'higher' status in the World of
COMPETITION!

Competitiveness – Yes!
Quickly now – take as much as you can, as quickly as you can,
to maintain a Lifestyle for your very own Personal, and Political
Agendas!

The route Home to God was ONCE paved in Gold – many
thought in the olden days.
Now the way home to God is via the ATM Machine – as the
very 'Essence' of our Soul cries for survival!
Help – I need more money to SURVIVE for another week –
another day – for some – another hour – another minute!

The interest rates increase dramatically, to accommodate the
overspending and free spending of OUR money – the taxpayers
money. Millions and billions of dollars soar skywards – for ALL
the Governments *think* we need.

Armies, Machinery, Nuclear Plants, Ships, Oil Wells, Mining
Rights – the list is never-ending.
Where does the money come from?
It comes from the 'average' person in the street, who has worked
hard, paid their taxes, and has NO say at all on what the
Government spending agenda is, has been, or will be!
Yes, we *think* we do – this is an illusion!
An illusion based on false realities, fed to us – like a Mother
spoon-feeding an infant.
AND WE EAT – WHAT WE ARE GIVEN!

The greed, hate and vengeance boil up within the very Core of
our Existence. We struggle and struggle to provide a living for

yet another day, and become disillusioned, and despondent, over the pressures of day-to-day living.

Yes, most live in an environment of *trapped* ABANDONMENT!

You lapse in your trust and faith in yourself, and your ability to provide for yourself and your family. You try to cut corners and manipulate your finances, to accommodate a lifestyle YOU THOUGHT YOU HAD!

As produce prices increase, land prices increase, housing prices increase, rents increase, taxes increase – Wages REMAIN basic and stagnant.

You never cease to be amazed when you read in the newspapers the building of a new 'Bridge' will cost one hundred million, or the new by-pass road billions of dollars.

The Governments huddle together, and strategize how to reap yet MORE money from the average person. The ones trying to have a life, keep a life – at any expense by now!

The struggle to survive is equally proportionate to the struggle of competitiveness – within the Governments of our Nations.

So we – the average – poor – struggle to survive.

They – the Governments or People in Power – struggle to survive on yet another level.

The only difference being – those in Power INCREASE their salaries in accordance with their struggle!

So struggle becomes the Very Core of Our Existence!

On a Godly Level – Survival is paramount for Existence – SURVIVAL OF THE FITTEST!

Are we fit?

You would have to laugh – Fit?

Exhausted from struggle maybe.

Despondent from struggle maybe.

Or living Death from struggle maybe.

Here we are only talking about the Humans who can manage to struggle and survive!

What about those who rely on their Governments for survival? THEY HAVE NO CHANCE OF SURVIVAL!

You give money to help the Institutions and Governments to feed, educate, and provide farming equipment and land – to help the poor help themselves.

How much of 'that' money is actually being spent?

Maybe $10.00 in every hundred?

Maybe $3.00 in every hundred?

Maybe $1.00 in every hundred?

How about 1-10 cents in every hundred, in some cases!

Where does the money go?

To accommodate and facilitate the lives of those in positions of Administration and Power!

Yes, yes, some actually work hard, no doubt about that, however, the overall structure of The World Health Organization is still – ALL ABOUT THEM!

Oh yes, they strategize, listen, and send others – The Ones WHO DO WORK HARD – here and there to facilitate health and healing.

Eventually a slow regeneration of Self begins – only to be thwarted once more by more wars, more famine, more death and destruction.

So as one Country *seems* to be 'developing' – another Country is being DESTROYED!

The balance has been brought back yet once again to – THE STRUGGLE FOR SURVIVAL!

Just another parent and child, another Country *this* time.

We *lose* FOCUS on 'that' problem, as we become absorbed in the 'new' problem.

No *real* Change has taken place – just another day of manipulation, famine, destruction, yet once again.

When the ebb of Human Nature reaches its LOWEST point – whether it be Religious, Political, Civil, Personal, Environmental, the despondency within the very Essence of Self almost ceases to exist!
There is no room for anything except – SURVIVAL OF THE FITTEST!

The destruction of Man and the Environment on the outside – Globally – equals the internal struggle of Man and the Environment on the inside – AN INTRA-CELLULAR STRUGGLE!

Survival is the Breath of Life for us.
We may utter the phrase – 'Please help me God!' in the midst of the Global and Personal confusion, as we confront a bottomless pit of misery!

Once one sinks to the depths – the depths of 'The Illusion of Despair' – it magnifies and solidifies, into a sewer of Self-Destructive ideas and agendas.
As this 'sewer' of negativity gains momentum, and we become entrenched and saturated within the confines of Negativity – the cost of Survival dominates our every thought. Eventually settling and spewing forth – physically, emotionally, psychically, spiritually.

We sink lower and lower, then eventually MINE THE DARK – our very own dark – from this lifetime and life times past.
The war and total destruction the Governments have instigated globally, are being reflected totally within 'our' cells – The Essence of Self.

When you *lose* your power to Live – vulnerability becomes a way of living, and this vulnerability is magnified to manipulate and CONTROL *this* Fear!

Fear and Control -- No different to Governments and Nations.

All fearful are controlled, or want to control others – the root of Domestic Violence?

Yes, a mirror reflection of our very Essence of Self!

The only ingredient missing is the mention of Wealth.

Control and Power, however only if Money is involved.

Remember – LOVE OF MONEY is the Root of ALL Evil!

The only difference between Governments and us – is the manipulation of their AGENDAS by Wealth or *supposed* Wealth.

We still have the same agendas – it is just that the poor have no money – the Governments do!

The poor still hanker for the money, power and control – TO OVERCOME THEIR FEAR!

When Man is starving – he will eat at WHOEVER'S table is FULL!

Maybe with good intentions at first, but to be surrounded by Negative ambition, is an area of IMBALANCE that overpowers the very senses of Man.

It lowers resistance, and permeates and invades the very Essence of Self. Resulting often in Self Destructive Patterning, Manipulation and Deceit.

Often, the final outcome – IS RETALIATION & RETRIBUTION or An Eye for an Eye!

When confronted with these Negative feelings of Self – The Dharmic Pattern of Your Existence, changes to accommodate the Global Patterning of Evolution.

The DNA of Man comes in to alignment with the Global Energies, Frequencies and Vibrations – they run as a concurrent!

216

IT IS AT THIS TIME YOU ARE AFFORDED THE OPPORTUNITY TO UTILISE AND ENJOY THE FRUITS OF YOUR HARD LABOUR BY – RECOGNIZING, RE-EVALUATING AND RELEASING – ALL NEGATIVE ASPECTS OF SELF – THE MIRROR OF MAYA – THE TRANSIENT, THE ILLUSIVE PERCEPTION OF 'WHO' WE THINK WE ARE!

Om Sai Ram.

THE
ATHI RUDRA
MAHA YAGNA – DAY 4

THE YAGNA – DAY 4: RECOGNITION.

12.08.06

Liberation of Self from Self.
Yes, it is all about 'Recognition.'
Just to recognize the extremes in Human Behaviour Patterning,
will activate a 'Form' of Release or the beginnings of Release.

After the Global Turmoil – the current level of increase in EFV
(Energies, Frequencies and Vibrations) invades our very essence.
We are forced to ACCEPT the 'new' levels of activity within
our own Essence of Self.
Due to Global EFV increase – we experience the Personal /
Human increase within a limited timeframe. Some say
simultaneously, however only if you are one of the few spiritually
prepared.

By 'preparation' it is meant – those Beings out there that already
have accommodated and mastered the areas of Spiritual
Frequency Sliding Scale. Some say – The Spiritual Elite –

however 'elitism' is a pride based Negative imbalance, that will not sustain the very Essence of Man.
It is Ego driven and Ego based!

As the Negative Energies – both Global and Personal, activate our very existence and provide us with the AWARENESS to facilitate CHANGE – we must observe with due diligence and great care – what it is we are actually experiencing.

We must listen to our 'Inner Voice,' and observe all aspects of our Physicality! Feel our emotions, and only if necessary, experience the Negativity oozing from the very depths of our Soul. Allow 'Recognition' to take place.
Only in and through this 'Trial by Fire,' will we be truly able to seek refuge within our Soul – the very Essence of our Being.

Do not 'temper' or lessen the pain, exhaustion, distaste – brewing up inside our minds and hearts at this time.
Experience ALL aspects of Self – Negative as they may be at that time.
This the *true* way to Salvation of the Soul.

Recognize and Experience!
Through the Recognition, will flow the Experience – through the Experience will flow the Release!

Your heart is a continual well of love, when cleansed and open to receive the love of God. The love of God from within, will flow on to the whole of humanity.
Humanity is waiting to receive the love from another.
Remember - LOVE ENGENDERS LOVE.

Do not be righteous or pious – if you had not sinned in Past Lives – you would not be here on Earth at this time. So no judgement should ever take place.

No judgement of other Nations, Countries, People – or so God says.
God says – Who are YOU to Judge?
However, how difficult it is NOT to judge!
The innocent are being slaughtered,
Homes and lands devastated by war and invasion – and still God says – Do not Judge!

Open your heart – After ACCEPTING the massive increase in Global EFV, and still further ACCEPT the increase in the Human EFV as well.
Then ALLOW yourself to experience all 'negative' qualities within the Environment and Humanity in general, and ACCEPT further the 'negative' feelings, and Global and Personal Self Destructive Patterning.

So we not only have to Recognize, but we have to ACCEPT as well?
Yes, all must ACCEPT - THE WILL OF GOD.
This is God's time to sort out Humanity – and in time – God's time – the Wheat from the Chaff!

The Chaff you think will be weak – the Wheat strong?
This is all an illusion – sometimes, as with nature – the wheat will be spoilt – damaged from the ravages of nature or disease.
This is now what you are all seeing, and experiencing.

You *look* at your 'Crop of Wheat' as a rare jewel – a way of survival, a source of food or fodder – A MEANS TO AN END!
'Wheat' can save you – however only if the 'Will of God' allows this to occur.

You *think* of 'Chaff' as second rate!
Not necessarily so either!

The animals can be fed, baskets can be woven, objects made, homes built, fires can be maintained.
So chaff can be a mainstay as well as wheat.

To separate the Wheat from the Chaff is a daunting encumbrance for the mainstay of existence, and the survival of Man.
Great strength of character needs to be maintained to achieve this almighty feat.

Once again – No Judgement should ever take place.
ALL IS IN THE DIVINE LEDGER AND DIVINE AGENDA.

Om Sai Ram.

THE
ATHI RUDRA
MAHA YAGNA – DAY 5

THE YAGNA – DAY 5: RELEASE.

13.08.06

Release ALL thoughts of Self!
Do not pass Judgements on /of others.
Liberation is just around the corner!

This morning I observed the chaos in Israel, Lebanon, Pakistan
and Iraq, then listening to the news of The World on the BBC –
about the terrorism in the UK and America, followed by a replay
of The Regime in Argentina, and the lost children.
Then yesterday a program yet once again on The Holocaust
and the survivors, and their stories and interpretations.
So still more news on death and destruction to heighten yet once
again the FEARS of the average person.

To Live in Fear – is to Die in Fear!

It appears that War is a Collective Consciousness!
It gathers momentum and speed, until ALL are involved.

Not just Governments and Nations, but the people in the street, and the workers in the fields.

People here and there – all have loved ones, family, friends, acquaintances, trapped here or there.
Either imprisoned on the inside through terror or fear – or imprisoned on the outside through control and extremist deprivation of liberties.
We are ALL surrounded by Fear!
Fear – here, there, everywhere!

So how do we overcome this Fear?
Easy!
Just as before, we have to tenderly embrace the very Negative aspect of Self, until it begins to resonate with the very Essence of our Being.
How can it resonate you ask?
It can, and will resonate with Self, so long as the 'Fear' itself - is surrounded and embraced by LOVE. The love that exudes from the very heart of Man. The love that can rebuild a war torn area to a place of great beauty.
The hearts of ALL men are Pure and Untainted – IT IS THE PHYSICAL ASPECT OF SELF – THE EGO – THAT RULES THE MORAL CODE AND BEHAVIOUR OF MAN!

To enter a war torn area, a place of terrorism, a place of devastation – is still only a 'mirror' of the terrorism and devastation we are currently experiencing in our cells.
The ravages of war and extremist behaviour are taking a toll on Man and his Civil Liberties, however this is ONLY possible as long as we remain ENTRENCHED IN FEAR!

Fear is only ONE area of the Negative Aspect of Self!
Are we not two parts of the Whole?
Positive and Negative!

The light of God shines stronger and more potent - than the darkness pervading the Earth at this time.

So the answer to this problem is –

SEND MORE LIGHT IN ABUNDANCE – TO ALL!

The Terrorists, the Governments, the People in places of Power, who are still damaging with destructive force – the innocent People, their Countries, and the Environment in which they have been forced to live!

PRAY AND SEND MORE LIGHT – THAT TRULY IS THE ULTIMATE FORM OF RELEASE.

RELEASE BECOMES FREEDOM WHEN THESE PRINCIPLES ARE APPLIED WITH AND FROM A LOVING HEART!

Om Sai Ram.

THE
ATHI RUDRA
MAHA YAGNA – DAY 6

THE YAGNA – DAY 6: REJUVENATION.

14.08.06

'Rejuvenation' is a loose term enjoyed and bandied around by the social elite, and the superior Consciousness of Man.
APPEARANCE AND HEALTH!
Rejuvenation of Self, as we search and search still more, for a way to lighten or reduce the load of 'aging' within our cells – and the very Essence of Being – our totality – our Physical Aspect of Self!

The choices are many and varied as we continually research and search yet once again, for the answer to the age-old question, 'What can WE do to reduce, limit, decrease, the aging within our physicality'?
The Appearance of Man – Yes we are once again back to The Ego!
Yes, many out there try to assimilate a well thought out exercise and nourishment regime, into the structure of their daily existence, and many do not.

Are these so called fitness and health conscious men and women filled to the brim with love for their fellow man, their country, and others living in destitute – in abhorrent conditions – elsewhere in the World?

Others from and in, the war torn and terrorist areas we have mentioned previously?

Is there anyway Seva / Service can be utilized to help in the proliferation of Cosmic Cleansing through the activation of LOVE?

By shining just 'one' light towards the ultimate form of RELIEF AND RELEASE - surely this would eventually be the most positive outcome for Humanity and the Planet at this time.

A peaceful and loving existence within the parameters of health, education and wellbeing, for the millions of others on the Planet, not to mention the Animals and the Environment.

Rejuvenation of Self by Self - that is the answer to the question of aging gracefully, or is it 'aging' with, and in the grace of, and from God?

Rejuvenation of Self becomes apparent when the word, thought and deed, of the very action and reaction of Man – begins to penetrate the Essence of the Soul of Man.

Rejuvenation of The God Self is what we are all trying to valiantly accomplish – NOT the Human Self – THE GOD SELF!

And how do we accomplish this?

By learning, listening, and adhering to – the most importance Principles of Life – Life Qualities – if you like.

And what are these Life Qualities you ask?

Just one set of Guidelines or Rules set out as the Basic Principles of Life – The 5 Human Values of – Truth, Righteous Conduct, Peace, Love and Non-Violence.

When and if these 5 Human Values are adhered to –
TRUE REJUVENATION OF SELF CAN TRULY BEGIN IN
EARNEST!

The Last 5 Days of THE YAGNA are the most *important* days,
and represent the 5 HUMAN VALUES or Life Principles of
Man – Truth, Righteousness, Peace, Love, and Non-violence.

THE
ATHI RUDRA
MAHA YAGNA – DAY 7

THE YAGNA – DAY 7: TRUTH – SATHYA.

15.08.06

Truth - The 1ˢᵗ Human Value.

Truth is a PURE Manifestation of Love.
There is no greater Truth than Love, and no greater Love than Truth.
They are, and have always been, intrinsically linked together as ONE. However let us now look at just 'plain' truth!

Many say – I want the plain truth, the real truth, the actual truth!
Truth, truth – there is only ONE TRUTH – God's Truth!
God's Truth is insurmountable in its abundance to try to capture and emulate – the TRUE Nature of Mankind.

Animals and Plants are always in THEIR Truth; it is the Human variety of existence that has the real problem of separating their Truth, from God's Truth!

Human Truth is a manifestation of The Ego – The my, mine, yours, ours, his, hers, or the *infamous* 'I'!

We wander around in varying degrees of 'lost' Consciousness CLAIMING *this* truth or *that* truth.
However the reality of the illusion is that 'our' truth is a pure and simple form of SEPARATION from God – NOT AN ALIGNMENT with God – as we would wish for it to be.

It is not intentional – no – but from the first moments of a child's life – we all try to infuse our opinions and truth on that child. 'Our' opinions and truth are just that – OURS!

Oh yes – we all proclaim we are giving them values, life lessons, teaching, loving, caring – the list is endless, however the one truth is – we are teaching them all – OUR TRUTH!
Where is *their* Truth?
Their Truth is guarded and hidden deep within the crevices of their Soul. It is never asserted, as it never had to be – for preservation – like animal instincts.
So THEIR Truth is smothered by OUR Truth.
From childhood – the battle begins!
Our Truth – the adult – over-riding their Truth – the child.
Whose Truth will win?
Not *their* Truth!
Well – let us say – NOT YET!

Eventually when the Soul Essence is totally out of alignment with the Cosmic Realization of Truth – then and only then 'our' children WILL TRY TO ASSERT THEIR TRUTH – or their version of the Truth.
It is only when *this* assertion really formulates – the action and reaction of Truth, begins to take place.

In the mighty struggle that ensues – the 'internal' struggle for truth, versus the 'external' struggle for acknowledgement – existence. It is only then – Truth of *some* degree or another, will surely win out!

Struggle, then acknowledgement of The True Self hopefully emerges!
As the struggle and search for the 'true' Self continues, one is capable of discovering at this time THEIR Truth – THE TRUTH, God's Truth – the actual Truth of the reality of the illusion to, of, and for Life. Maybe even the answer to the most important question of existence – the answer to – 'Who' am I Really?

As the struggle continues and deepens – the crevices of our Soul begin to reconnect and recognize once more, its very own Essence – Truth – Soul Truth.
When we connect directly to our Soul Truth, the 'truth' becomes a part of our everyday existence.

The Monkey Mind – the Ego – begins to fade back into oblivion, AS WE PROCLAIM 'OUR' TRUTH – GOD'S TRUTH!

To attain the heights of Truth – one will open up a 'darker' aspect of Self – the Alter Ego!
Yet once again – another battle, another struggle for survival, or is it the same struggle?
Yes, it is the same – Our Truth – Ego – the darker side of our personality traits, has been the PROBLEM all along!
Yes, we have all been struggling against 'our' Truth – the Ego Truth – based on the 'I' of existence and survival some say!

How do we release the 'I' – the Ego?
Just utilise the 3 R's – Recognize, Re-evaluate and Release!
Yes, it is all about seeing – looking deeper into the crevices of our Monkey Mind, then releasing the Negative Aspect of Self

BY EMBRACING & RECLAIMING THAT PART OF YOU,
THAT PART YOU NO LONGER NEED, WANT OR DESIRE.

So love the Negative Aspect of Self with all your might, and
embrace Your Ego Self – and surround it with light and love – all
you can muster!
Only LOVE will set 'The Truth' FREE.
Then and only then – Your Truth and God's Truth –
WILL BE AS ONE!

Om Sai Ram.

THE
ATHI RUDRA
MAHA YAGNA – DAY 8

THE YAGNA – DAY 8: RIGHTEOUSNESS – DHARMA.

16.08.06

Righteous Conduct – The 2nd Human Value.

What exactly does 'this' Value represent?
In many, it represents Aims and Goals – a very positive aspect of Creation and Man – or so one would think!

Aims and Goals are both infused within the parameters of once again – the Monkey Mind – the Ego.
As the true aim or goal of Life is but a simple one – To be present in the here and NOW!

To be present in the NOW, allows us the opportunity to live moment to moment.
Only in the moment do we forget or obliterate aims and goals as a thought wave or parallel of 'supposition' – a Negative form of thought.

To be present, and allow 'the Truth' to immerse the very Essence of Self, then reflect *this* Truth onwards – into the wider areas of life, as a Divine Reflection of Self – this surely is The Golden Aim!
Because only in Truth, with Truth, can we attain and maintain RIGHTEOUS CONDUCT OR RIGHTEOUSNESS.

Righteousness cannot occur in the *absence* of Truth.
Truth is Righteousness – if delivered and utilized within the bounds of Righteous Conduct.

When the level of our Moral Code is lessened, by the continual and perpetual aims and goals of Man and his Monkey Mind or Ego – Righteousness becomes no longer apparent, or in some cases – cannot under any circumstances be executed with due diligence.

Righteous Conduct requires TRUTH as the mainstay of stability.
It aligns itself with a Moral, Ethical, Spiritual Code, in the power of Acceptance of NOW!
We learn how to conduct ourselves in purity and truth, for the betterment of Mankind and the Environment.

When we live in Truth, then all actions will be Righteous.
This may *not* appear to be the case! However if truth hurts – it is only the Ego that has been bruised – NOT the heart of Man.

So all Righteous Conduct and Actions affecting the Ego of Man may 'appear' to not have a positive effect. However ALL is positive, as it allows TRANSITION to occur – another lesson to be learnt, another gate to open, another pillar to fall!

Some 'think' their actions are performed in Righteousness.
Righteousness for whom?

Them?
Yes, for some!
There is NO transference of GRACE.

God bestows numerous favours of Grace upon many!
Grace is a commodity that requires only one thing to help uplift
Humanity – TRANSFERENCE!

With 'Transference' – God bestows Grace upon his fellow Man,
allowing him / her to then transfer 'that' Grace on to the rest of
Humanity.
Does this occur?
Seldom!
Most who receive Grace – bathe in the bliss of 'that' grace.
They see it as THEIRS' – not necessarily as a proliferation to
and for others to receive.

When Grace is prevented or stopped from transferring, through
or due to many and varied circumstances, then the grace received
REBOUNDS – and causes a Molecular Imbalance within the
cells of our being.

To withhold Grace – leads to a cruel form of 'separation' from
The God Force or God Energy.
This eventuates and perpetuates into deeper feelings of 'lack.'
So even though this person KNOWS they are truly receiving
grace from God, they actually feel as though they are NOT!
On a mental level KNOW this to be a pure truth – RECEIVING
GRACE.
On a heart level KNOW they are incapable of ACCEPTING
GRACE!

The main prerequisite for Righteous Conduct is Truth
accompanied by the Transference of Grace.

Only in the 'Transference of Grace,' can one attain the mastery of Righteous Conduct in ALL areas and aspects of life. Be it Human, Animal, Environmental.

Righteous Conduct occurs when TRUTH is present – and in that Truth – the GRACE transfers to enable Righteousness to occur with relative ease.

Om Sai Ram.

THE
ATHI RUDRA
MAHA YAGNA – DAY 9

THE YAGNA – DAY 9: PEACE – SHANTI.

17.08.06

Peace - The 3ʳᵈ Human Value.

Peace or Pieces?
Just how difficult is it to obtain, maintain, and then remain in a
State of Peace?
Almost an impossibility, or so it would appear to many.

Peace – or to be able to 'access' a place of Peace, can be an
illusive dream for some, and yet a definite possibility for a select
few.
Who are those 'supposedly' select few?
They are the evolved Souls who have been given the gift of
reincarnation at this time on Earth.
Why is this so?
To help restore the balance back to the three Worlds – and the
struggling Souls who inhabit the Earth at this time.

These special Souls have the ability to follow and accept the Golden Rule – Past is Past!
Remember – to Live in the Past – is to Die in the Past!

Meditation, Prayers, Service to Humanity and the Environment in general, is foremost in their hearts. To help facilitate health and healing to all levels of Humanity and the Environment, is a necessary part of their Soul Evolution at this time.

We all ponder – How can we proclaim to be in a State of Peace? First of all, Truth must be maintained.
Within the flow of Truth, we then experience the 'Grace of God.' Within this Grace, then of course Righteousness becomes our Moral Code of Conduct.

In experiencing Truth and Righteousness – an overwhelming feeling of Peace will begin to saturate the very Essence of our Soul.
Peace is a graduation into the formal commitment of Excellence, held within the internal search for the God Self.

As we absorb the Essence of Truth and Righteousness within the Core of our Being, our heart begins to open, and the Truth and Righteousness from within, expands into a deeper sense of Self. We expand our Consciousness, and then reflect our Truth yet once again. It is in this expansion, we begin to FEEL the flow of 'true' PEACE.

Peace passes through our every cell in a flow of caressing Energy. It then stimulates an experience from deep within of 'surrender' or a momentary lapse in judgements and Negative imbalance. Then as the Energy of Peace deepens, it continues on – as an overwhelming Energy of Love.

ONLY WHEN PEACE IS MAINTAINED WITHIN THE
SOUL OF ALL MANKIND WILL WARS, TERRORISM,
CATASTROPHES, DEVASTATION, POVERTY, FAMINE
AND DROUGHT, CEASE TO EXIST!

Our bellies will be full, or our Hearts will become full, as Peace
permeates the Core of our very Existence, and then generates
outward – towards the greater Universes, and all they stand for.

Wars, terrorism, famine, drought, are only ever a Divine
Reflection of The Internal Struggle of Man.
War on the INSIDE or lack of Peace, equates to war on the
OUTSIDE and *still* lack of Peace!

Only in the surrendering of One's Ego, by the activation of Truth
and Righteous Conduct – can one truly experience the emotions,
feelings and bliss of TRUE Peace.

Peace is a 'surrogate' Form of Love.
The feeling of – 'You are almost there – but not quite as yet!'

Peace is a lifeline that can be handicapped by poor Judgement.
Who are we to Judge?
No judgement should ever take place!
We do not know what past Karmas have instigated various
behaviour patterning.
Judgement, for and of others is one of the foremost causes of
'lack' of Peace.
Judgement is the mainstay of Negative Imbalance and
disempowerment of Man.
You Judge – You are Judged!
You may experience *some* areas of Truth and Righteous Conduct,
however if Judgement crosses your path and bounds into your
life, then Peace will evade the very core of your Existence.

Remember to experience Peace – No judgement should ever take place.

Peace is Non Judgement –
Peace is TRUTH AND RIGHTEOUSNESS.
Most of all – Peace is a necessary ingredient to enable us to experience and propagate – LOVE!

Om Sai Ram.

'Judge not, that ye be not judged, for with what judgement ye judge, so shall ye be judged.'

Matthew – The Holy Bible.

THE
ATHI RUDRA
MAHA YAGNA – DAY 10

THE YAGNA – DAY 10: LOVE – PREMA.

18.08.06

Love - The 4th Human Value.

Love is all there is – because Love transcends ALL Bounds –
colour, caste and creed.
Love is limitless in its intent. It soars where only Eagles dare to
soar – reaching the true heights of Man!
It has a numerical equivalent of – All there is!

Love is a compilation of Truth, Righteousness, and Peace.
Through the other 3 Human Values we can attain, and then
maintain - the flow of LOVE!

Love is within the Hearts and Souls of ALL men.
Love is Universal in its intent.
The great Beauty of Love is likened to –
The birth of a Child
A natural wonder of the World
An exhausting and yet fulfilling Search
A miraculous Discovery.

It is then we achieve the TRUE abundance we have all been searching for – LOVE!

Love fills the 'empty' Vessels of our sullied Hearts. It then turns our Hearts into pure - unsullied organs of bliss – Ananda!
Love conquers all – or so the saying goes.
This is a PURE Truth!

All wars, terrorist activities, famine and drought - ALL CEASE TO EXIST IN THE PRESENCE OF LOVE!
Why?
Because we all become ONE – ONE WITH UNIVERSAL INTENT!

There can be no wars when Man truly loves his brother.
The poor cannot die from hunger or thirst – as the wealthy share their monetary gains to help in the upliftment of Humanity.
This is a 'pure' Truth!
HOWEVER is this an actuality?
No!

Man hungers yet still for Power, Money and Control.
Governments are still creating waves of confusion, and producing macro-abusive substances to eliminate their 'so-called' Enemies.
Who are these Enemies?
Are they not their mother, father, brother or sister?
Yes, this is so.

How long before we all become ONE?
How long before we all LOVE instead of HATE?
When we are reduced to a 'zero' population?
When all of the animals have been annihilated?
When all of the trees obliterated?

How long before we learn to CLOSE that angry, abusive, jealous, selfish side of our Human Nature, and begin to act as DIVINE, as truly Divine Beings!

After all, are we not God?
I think so.

So if in fact we are – then why is our Heart CLOSED to our Divine Nature?
Is it because of the CONTROL AND SURVIVAL of The Monkey Mind – The Ego?
Yes, this is truth!
Does the Ego still lie deep within the crevices of your being?

Love abounds and is bountiful in ALL Human Beings.
Why not try to experience this state of bliss NOW?
Why wait?
What are you waiting FOR?
Time is passing or is it Life you are wasting?

To attain World Peace, we first have to implement Truth and Righteousness, and then Peace flows through to the very Core of our Existence. From this peace emanates the deep Love we are all waiting to experience.
Not an 'external' Love – mother – daughter – husband – wife.
This worldly love cannot be fulfilled with material desires!
The Golden Aim is for 'internal' Love - THE LOVE OF GOD!
Love of God is all that is important!
There is no greater love – than the Love of God.

All aspects of internal love – Love of God – beautifies, and distinguishes itself by obliterating all evil qualities from Man.
At present we are surrounded by many with negative thoughts, actions and deeds!
What are we to do?
Send them MORE Love!
ONLY LOVE CAN FREE THE VERY SOUL OF MAN.

Om Sai Ram.

THE
ATHI RUDRA
MAHA YAGNA – DAY 11

THE YAGNA – DAY 11: NON-VIOLENCE – AHIMSA.

19.08.06

Non-violence – The 5th Human Value.

The last of the 5 Human Values or Life Principles, that has the capacity to ultimately change the tide and flow of Violence in, with, and for Humanity, and all areas of Universal Understanding.

After instilling the 'other' Human Values into the very Essence of our totality – THIS VALUE OF NON-VIOLENCE becomes an accepted parameter, in the Divine flow of Light and Love.

When the other values have been attained and then maintained, then there is no acceptable way VIOLENCE CAN MATURE!

Violence within our cells alters our Molecular Vibration.
Violence?
Yes, any form of molecular instability creates mild to deep unrest within our Molecular Facilitation Break-up Process.

This unrest can inhibit or exacerbate the cellular activity, which alters the 'normal' range and rate of Molecular Restructuring taking place.

The deeper the anger, greed, arrogance, jealousy – the MORE violent the reaction and interaction, within our cells.

This Molecular imbalance can be responsible for many areas of illness or disease.

Over long periods of unsettled behaviour patterning, the Essence of Self begins to diminish in its intent, or the glow of Light from deep within ceases to exist at the optimum level – for Spiritual Growth or Spiritual Productivity.

It can be likened to ABANDONMENT OF THE ESSENCE OF SELF – OUR DIVINE RIGHT OF EXISTENCE.

We become 'disassociated' with our Divine Self, through the Negative Behaviour Patterning.

ALL THE NEGATIVE ASPECTS OR TRAITS OF HUMAN FRAILTY ARE ONLY MANIFESTATIONS OF ATTEMPTS AT SURVIVAL – COMPOUNDED & RE-COMPOUNDED, BY THE STRENGTH OF THE MONKEY MIND – THE EGO!

The Ego is the BUILDING block of Material success – Money, Power, Control, and the STUMBLING block for Awareness and Spiritual Growth.

In actual fact – The Ego is the ONE COMPLEX BLOCK that Self identifies with the 'darker' aspect of the Essence of Self.

In most cases the darker aspect of Self – the Ego – reigns supreme!

Often in a quiet, discreet, apparently non-violent way, however often in an overt, aggressive more violent way.

The Ego is directly out of alignment with OUR Highest Good!

The Ego is the 'root cause' of Negative Behaviour Patterning, and many forms of ill-health and disease.
The Molecular imbalance creates havoc within our cells, or in other words – INTERNAL VIOLENCE!
This 'violence' is projected outwards, and expands energetically in its INTENT!
The self made negative patterning of Man, self reflects, and self ejects.
The Energy of Negativity expands and blossoms forth, into ALL areas of life – our life – others' lives.

Wars, terrorism, famine, droughts, corruption, deceit, manipulation, are all areas of behaviour we see and experience daily in the media.

THEY ARE THE EXTERNAL MANIFESTATIONS OF THE INTERNAL STRUGGLE OF MAN.

When the internal Struggle of Man is provided with 'Food for the Soul' – by consuming as Nourishment – The 4 Human Values:
TRUTH
RIGHTEOUSNESS
PEACE
LOVE
then the 5th Human Value of NON-VIOLENCE becomes the MAINSTAY of our Society, and Liberation of the TRUE Self!

When Love abounds in the hearts of ALL Men, then Non-violence reigns supreme!
True and eternal bliss can only be acquired through LOVE.
And through that Love – Non-violence perpetuates and flows onwards, to the rest of Humanity.
Only in the presence of Love – the Negative Aspect of Man will CEASE to exist forever.

LOVE is the thread that binds The 5 Human Values together.
LOVE in speech is TRUTH
LOVE in action is RIGHTEOUSNESS
LOVE in thought is PEACE
LOVE in understanding is NON-VIOLENCE.

LOVE IS ALL THERE IS!

Om Sai Ram!

ABOUT THE AUTHOR

The Author was born near Rosslyn Chapel in Scotland. At an early age her family moved to Australia where her search to discover 'The Meaning of Life' began in earnest.

Irene has travelled to many countries of Spiritual Significance including Egypt, Peru, Tibet, Easter Island, Mexico, and *specific* areas in Great Britain, Europe and USA. Finally the journey took her to India where she discovered 'The Jewel in the Crown' Sri Sathya Sai Baba.

In 2006, Irene travelled throughout India visiting The 12 Jyotir Lingams, and to The Holy Mt. Kailash in Tibet – the abode of Lord Shiva and Goddess Parvathi – to participate in the Parikrama – the 56 kilometer trek around the base of Mt. Kailash.

Irene continues to bond with India as she interacts with Sri Sathya Sai Baba and The Divine Mother – Srimad Sai Rajarajeshwari, in their endeavors to instill the five Human Values of Truth, Righteousness, Peace, Love, and Non-violence globally.

Janice Harvey, Author
'One Stone for Tibet' &
'Mum, it's nothing personal, but I want to die.'